SEED LEGISLATION

SEED LEGISLATION

Editor

Premjit Sharma

2008

Gene-Tech Books

New Delhi - 110 002

ISBN10 81-89729-88-8
ISBN13 978-81-89729-88-2

Published by : **GENE-TECH BOOKS**
4762-63/23, Ansari Road, Darya Ganj,
NEW DELHI - 110 002
Phone: 41562849
e-mail: genetechbooks@yahoo.co.in

Printed at : **Tarun Offset Printers**
Delhi

PRINTED IN INDIA

Preface

Seed production and distribution involves judicious effort of the producer and the enforcement agency. The job of the seed producer becomes ever more important today, as he is the vital link between the lab and the land. A majority of the farming community being semi literate or illiterate in India, the owes of providing a framework that governs production and distribution of quality seeds lies on the shoulders of the government.

With the flooding of sub-standard and inferior quality of seeds in the market, it has become extremely crucial for the seed producer to follow rules and regulations so as not to adversely affect the agricultural output. 'Seed legislation' is therefore an effort to familiarise the reader with the various procedures involved in seed law enforcement.

This book guides the reader on the various seed production schemes and certifications validated by the Government of India in order to improve the farmers' working capacity in the field. It introduces the various standards in seed testing and seed legislation, and elaborates on those standards deemed necessary by the government to regulate registration, selection, storage, transfer and use of seed. It also explains the various legislatives, acts and laws passed by the testing, inspection, quality and sale of seeds. All in all being a comprehensive guide into the issue, it is hoped that this book proves highly useful to seed producers and agriculturalists.

Premjit Sharma

Contents

1

The Seeds Act, 1966

(Act No.54 of 1966)

[29th December, 1966]

An Act to provide for regulating the quality of certain seeds for sale, and for matters connected therewith.

BE it enacted by Parliament in the Seventeenth Year of the Republic of India as follows:

Short Title, Extent and Commencement

1.(1) This Act may be called the Seeds Act, 1966.

(2) It extends to the whole of India.

(3) It shall come into force on such date as the Central Government may, by notification in the Official Gazette, appoint, and different dates may be appointed for different provisions of this Act, and for different States or for different areas thereof.

Definitions

2. In this Act, unless the context otherwise requires,

(1) "Agriculture" includes horticulture;

(2) "Central Seed Laboratory" means the Central Seed Laboratory established or declared as such

under sub-section (1) of section 4;(3) "Certification agency" means the certification agency established

(4) "Committee" means the Central Seed Committee constituted under sub-section (1) of Section 3;

(5) "Container" means a box, bottle, casket, tin, barrel, case, receptacle, sack, bag, wrapper or other thing in which any article or thing is placed or packed;

(6) "Export" means taking out of India to a place outside India;

(7) "Import" means bringing into India from a place outside India;

(8) "Kind" means one or more related species or sub-species of crop plants each individually or collectively known by one common name such as cabbage, maize, paddy and wheat;

(9) "notified kind or variety" , in relation to any seed, means any kind or variety thereof notified under Section 5;

(10) "Prescribed" means prescribed by rules made under this act;

(11) "seed" means any of the following classes of seeds used for sowing or planting-

(i) seeds of food crops including edible oil seeds and seeds of fruits and vegetables;

(ii) cotton seeds;

(iii) seeds of cattle fodder;and includes seedlings, and tubers, bulbs, rhizomes, roots, cuttings, all types of grafts and other vegetatively propagated material, of food crops or cattle fodder;

(12) "Seed Analyst" means a Seed Analyst appointed under section 12;

(13) "Seed Inspector" means a Seed Inspector appointed under section 13;

(14) "State Government", in relation to a Union territory, means the administrator thereof;

(15) "State Seed Laboratory", in relation to any State, means the State Seed Laboratory established or declared as such under sub-section (2) of section 4 for that State; and

(16) "variety" means a sub-division of a kind identifiable by growth, yield, plant, fruit, seed, or other characteristic.

Central Seed Committee

3.(1) The Central Government shall, as soon as may be after the commencement of this Act, constitute a Committee called the Central Seed Committee to advise the Central Government and the State Governments on matters arising out of the administration of this Act and to carry out the other functions assigned to it by or under this Act.

(2) The Committee shall consist of the following members, namely:-

(i) a Chairman to be nominated by the Central Government;

(ii) eight persons to be nominated by the Central Government to represent such interests that Government thinks fit, of whom not less than two persons shall be representatives of growers of seed;

(iii) one person to be nominated by the Government of each of the States.

(3) The members of the Committee shall, unless their seats become vacant earlier by resignation, death or otherwise, be entitled to hold office for two years and shall be eligible for renomination.

(4) The Committee may, subject to the previous approval of the Central Government, make bye-laws fixing the quorum and regulating its own procedure and the conduct of all business to be transacted by it.

(5) The Committee may appoint one or more sub-committees, consisting wholly of members of the Committee or wholly of other persons or partly of members of the Committee and partly of other persons, as it thinks fit, for the purpose of discharging such of its functions as may be delegated to such sub-committee or sub-committees by the Committee.

(6) The functions of the Committee or any sub-committee thereof may be exercised notwithstanding any vacancy therein.

(7) The Central Government shall appoint a person to be the secretary of the Committee and shall provide the Committee with such clerical and other staff as the Central Government considers necessary.

Central Seed Laboratory and State Seed Laboratory

4.(1) The Central Government may, by notification in the Official Gazette, establish a Central Seed Laboratory or declare any seed laboratory as the Central Seed Laboratory to carry out the functions entrusted to the Central Seed Laboratory by or under this Act.

(2) The State Government may, by notification in the Official Gazette, establish one or more State Seed Laboratories or declare any seed laboratory as a State Seed Laboratory where analysis of seeds of any notified kind or variety shall be carried out by Seed Analysts under this Act in the prescribed manner.

Regulation of Sale of Seeds of Notified Kinds or Varieties

7. No person shall, himself or by any other person on his behalf, carry on the business of selling, keeping for sale, offering to sell, bartering or otherwise supplying any seed of any notified kind or variety, unless-

(a) such seed is identifiable as to its kind or variety;

(b) such seed conforms to the minimum limits of germination and purity specified under clause (a) of section 6;

(c) the container of such seed bears in the prescribed manner, the mark or label containing the correct particulars thereof, specified under clause (b) of section 6; and

(d) he complies with such other requirements as may be prescribed.

Certification Agency

8. The State Government or the Central Government in consultation with the State Government may, by notification in the Official Gazette, establish a certification agency for the State to carry out the functions entrusted to the certification agency by or under this Act.

Grant of Certificate by Certification Agency

9. (1) Any person selling, keeping for sale, offering to sell, bartering or otherwise supplying any seed of any notified kind or variety may, if he desires to have such seed certified by the certification agency, apply to the certification agency for the grant of a certificate for the purpose.

(2) Every application under sub-section (1) shall be made in such form, shall contain such particulars and shall be accompanied by such fees as may be prescribed.

(3) On receipt of any such application for the grant of a certificate, the certification agency may, after such enquiry as it thinks fit and after satisfying itself that the seed to which the application relates conforms to the minimum limits of germination and purity specified for that seed under clause (a) of section 6, grant a certificate in such form and on such conditions as may be prescribed.

Revocation of Certificate

10. If the certification agency is satisfied, either on a reference made to it in this behalf or otherwise, that-

(a) the certificate granted by it under section 9 has been obtained by misrepresentation as to an essential fact; or

(b) the holder of the certificate has, without reasonable cause, failed to comply with the conditions subject to which the certificate has been granted or has contravened any of the provisions of this Act or the rules made thereunder; then, without prejudice to any other penalty to which the holder of the certificate may be liable under this Act, the certification agency may, after giving the holder of the certificate an opportunity of showing cause, revoke the certificate.

Appeal

11(1) Any person aggrieved by a decision of a certification agency under section 9 or section 10, may, within thirty days from the date on which the decision is communicated to him and on payment of such fees as may be prescribed, prefer an appeal to such authority as may be specified by the State Government in this behalf: Provided that the appellate authority may entertain an appeal after the expiry of the said period of thirty days if it is satisfied that the appellate was prevented by sufficient cause from filing the appeal in time.

(2) On receipt of an appeal under sub-section (1), the appellate authority shall, after giving the appellant an opportunity of being heard, dispose of the appeal as expeditiously as possible.

(3) Every order of the appellate authority under this section shall be final.

Seed Analysts

12. The State Government may, by notification in the Official Gazette, appoint such persons as it thinks fit, having the prescribed qualifications, to be Seed Analysts and define the areas within which they shall exercise jurisdiction.

Seed Inspectors

13.(1) The State Government may, by notification in the Official Gazette, appoint such persons as it thinks fit, having the prescribed qualifications, to be Seed Inspectors and define the areas within which they shall exercise jurisdiction.

(2) Every Seed Inspector shall be deemed to be a public servant within the meaning of section 21 of the Indian Penal Code (45 of 1860) and shall be officially subordinate to such authority as the State Government may specify in this behalf.

Powers of Seed Inspector

14.(1) The Seed Inspector may-

(a) take samples of any seed of any notified kind or variety from-

(i) any person selling such seed; or

(ii) any person who is in the course of conveying, delivering or preparing to deliver such seed to a purchaser or a consignee; or

(iii) a purchaser or a consignee after delivery of such seed to him;

(b) send such sample for analysis to the Seed Analyst for the area within which such sample has been taken;

(c) enter and search at all reasonable times, with such assistance, if any, as he considers necessary, any place in which he has reason to believe that an offence under this Act has been or is being committed and order in writing the person in possession of any seed in respect of which the offence has been or is being committed, not to dispose of any stock of such seed for a specific period not exceeding thirty days or, unless the alleged offence is such that the defect may be removed by the possessor of the seed, seize the stock of such seed;

(d) examine any record, register, document or any other material object found in any place mentioned in clause (c) and seize the same if he has reason to believe that it may furnish evidence of the commission of an offence punishable under this Act; and

(e) exercise such other powers as may be necessary for carrying out the purposes of this Act or any rule made thereunder.

(2) Where any sample of any seed of any notified kind or variety is taken under clause (a) of sub-section (1), its cost, calculated at the rate at which such seed is usually sold to the public, shall be paid on demand to the person from whom it is taken.

(3) The power conferred by this section includes power to break-open any container in which any seed of any notified kind or variety may be contained or to break-open the door of any premises where any such seed may be kept for sale:

Provided that the power to break-open the door shall be exercised only after the owner or any other person in occupation of the premises, if he is present therein, refuses to open the door on being called upon to do so.

(4) Where the Seed Inspector takes any action under clause (a) of sub-section (1), he shall, as far as possible, call not less than two persons to be present at the time when such action is taken and take their signatures on a memorandum to be prepared in the prescribed form and manner.

(5) The provisions of the Code of Criminal Procedure, 1898 (5 of 1898), shall, so far as may be, apply to any search or seizure under this section as they apply to any search or seizure made under the authority of a warrant issued under section 98 of the said Code.

Procedure to be followed by Seed Inspectors

15.(1) Whenever a Seed Inspector intends to take sample of any seed of any notified kind or variety for analysis, he shall-

(a) give notice in writing, then and there, of such intention to the person from whom he intends to take sample;

(b) except in special cases provided by rules made under this Act, take three representative samples in the prescribed manner and mark and seal or fasten up each sample in such manner as its nature permits.

(2) When samples of any seed of any notified kind or variety are taken under sub-section (1), the Seed Inspector shall-

(a) deliver one sample to the person from whom it has been taken;

(b) send in the prescribed manner another sample for analysis to the Seed Analyst for the area within which such sample has been taken; and

(c) retain the remaining sample in the prescribed manner for production in case any legal proceedings are taken or for analysis by the Central Seed Laboratory under sub-section (2) of section 16, as the case may be.

(3) If the person from whom the samples have been taken refuses to accept one of the samples, the Seed Inspector shall send intimation to the Seed Analyst of such refusal and thereupon the Seed Analyst receiving the sample for analysis shall divide it into two parts and shall seal or fasten up one of those parts and shall cause it, either upon receipt of the sample or when he delivers his report, to be delivered to the Seed Inspector who shall retain it for production in case legal proceedings are taken.

(4) Where a Seed Inspector takes any action under clause (c) of sub-section (1) of section 14:

(a) he shall use all despatch in ascertaining whether or not the seed contravenes any of the provisions of section 7 and if it is ascertained that the seed does not so contravene, forthwith revoke the order passed under the said clause or, as the case may be, take such action as may be necessary for the return of the stock of the seed seized;

(b) if he seizes the stock of the seed, he shall, as soon as may be, inform a magistrate and take his orders as to the custody thereof;

(c) without prejudice to the institution of any prosecution, if the alleged offence is such that the defect may be removed by the possessor of the seed, he shall, on being satisfied that the defect has been so removed, forthwith revoke the order passed under the said clause.

(5) Where as Seed Inspector seizes any record, register, document or any other material object under clause (d) of sub-section (1) of section 14, he shall, as soon as may be, inform a magistrate and take his orders as to the custody thereof.

Report of Seed Analyst

16.(1) The Seed Analyst shall, as soon as may be after the receipt of the sample under sub-section (2) of section 15, analyse the sample at the State Seed Laboratory and deliver, in such form as may be prescribed, one copy of the report of the result of the analysis to the Seed Inspector and another copy thereof to the person from whom the sample has been taken.

(2) After the institution of a prosecution under this Act, the accused vendor or the complainant may, on payment of the prescribed fee, make an application to the court for sending any of the samples mentioned in clause (a) or clause (c) of sub-section (2) of section 15 to the Central Seed Laboratory for its report and on receipt of the application, the court shall first ascertain that the mark and the seal or fastening as provided in clause (b) of sub-section (1) of section 15 are intact and may then despatch the sample under its own seal to the Central Seed Laboratory which shall thereupon send its report to the court in the prescribed form within one month from the date of receipt of the sample, specifying the result of the analysis.

(3) The report sent by the Central Seed Laboratory under sub-section (2) shall supersede the report given by the Seed Analyst under sub-section (1).

(4) Where the report sent by the Central Seed Laboratory under sub-section (2) is produced in any proceedings under Section 19, it shall not be necessary in such proceedings to produce any sample or part thereof taken for analysis.

Restriction on Export and Import of Seeds of Notified kinds or Varieties

17. No person shall, for the purpose of sowing or planting by any person (including himself), export or import or cause to be exported or imported any seed of any notified kind or variety, unless-

(a) it conforms to the minimum limits of germination and purity specified for that seed under clause (a) of section 6; and

(b) its container bears, in the prescribed manner, the mark or label with the correct particulars thereof specified for that seed under clause (b) of section 6.

Recognition of Seed Certification Agencies of Foreign Countries

18. The Central Govt. may, on the recommendation of the Committee and by notification in the Official Gazette, recognise any seed certification agency established in any foreign country, for the purposes of this Act.

Penalty

19. If any person-

(a) contravenes any provision of this Act or any rule made thereunder; or

(b) prevents a Seed Inspector from taking sample under this Act;

or

(c) prevents a Seed Inspector from exercising any other power conferred on him by or under this Act; he shall, on conviction, be punishable-

(i) for the first offence with fine which may extend to five hundred rupees, and

(ii) in the event of such person having been previously convicted of an offence under this section, with imprisonment for a term which may extend to six months, or with fine which may extend to one thousand rupees, or with both.

Forfeiture of Property

20. When any person has been convicted under this Act for the contravention of any of the provisions of this Act or the rules made thereunder, the seed in respect of which the contravention has been committed may be forfeited to the Government.

Offences by Companies

21.(1) Where an offence under this Act has been committed by a company, every person who at the time the offence was committed was in charge of, and was responsible to the company for the conduct of the business of the company, as well as the company, shall be deemed to be guilty of the offence and shall be liable to be proceeded against and punished accordingly:

Provided that nothing contained in this sub-section shall render any such person liable to any punishment under this Act if he proves that the offence was committed without his knowledge and that he exercised all due diligence to prevent the commission of such offence.

(2) Notwithstanding anything contained in sub-section (1), where an offence under this Act has been committed by a company and it is proved that the offence has been committed with the consent or connivance of, or is attributable to any neglect on the part of, any director, manager, secretary or

other officer of the company, such director, manager, secretary or other officer shall also be deemed to be guilty of that offence and shall be liable to be proceeded against and punished accordingly.

Explanation:- For the purpose of this section,-

(a) "company" means any body corporate and includes a firm or other association of individuals; and

(b) "director", in relation to a firm, means a partner in the firm.

Protection of Action taken in Good Faith

22. No suit, prosecution or other legal proceeding shall lie against the Government or any officer of the Government anything which is in good faith done or intended to be done under this Act.

Power to give Directions

23. The Central Government may give such directions to any State Government as may appear to the Central Government to be necessary for carrying into execution in the State any of the provisions of this Act or of any rule made thereunder.

Exemption

24. Nothing in this Act shall apply to any seed of any notified kind or variety grown by a person and sold or delivered by him on his own premises direct to another person for being used by that person for the purpose of sowing or planting.

Power to make Rules

25.(1) The Central Government may, by notification in the

Official Gazette, make rules to carry out the purpose of this Act.

(2) In particular and without prejudice to the generality of the fore-going power, such rules may provide, for-

(a) the functions of the Committee and the travelling and daily allowances payable to members of the Committee and members of any sub-committee appointed under sub-section (5) of section 3;

(b) the functions of the Central Seed Laboratory;

(c) the functions of a certification agency;

(d) the manner of marking or labelling the container of seed of any notified kind or variety under clause (c) of Section 7 and under clause (b) of section 17;

(e) the requirements which may be complied with by a person carrying on the business referred to in section 7;

(f) the form of application for the grant of a certificate under section 9, the particulars it may contain, the fees which should accompany it, the form of the certificate and the conditions subject to which the certificate may be granted;

(g) the form and manner in which and the fee on payment of which an appeal may be preferred under section 11 and the procedure to be followed by the appellate authority in disposing of the appeal;

(h) the qualifications and duties of Seed Analysts and Seed Inspectors;

(i) the manner in which samples may be taken by the Seed Inspector, the procedure for sending such samples to the Seed Analyst or the Central Seed Laboratory and the manner of analysing such samples;

(j) the form of report of the result of the analysis under sub-section (1) or sub-section (2) of section 16 and the fees payable in respect of such report under the said sub-section (2);

(k) the records to be maintained by a person carrying on the business referred to in section 7 and the particulars which such records shall contain; and

(l) any other matter which is to be or may be prescribed.

(3) Every rule made under this Act shall be laid as soon as may be after it is made, before each House of Parliament while it is in session for a total period of thirty days which may be comprised in one session or in two successive sessions, and if, before the expiry of the session in which it is so laid or the session immediately following, both Houses agree in making any modification in the rule or both Houses agree that the rule should not be made, that rule shall, thereafter have effect only in such modified form or be of no effect, as the case may be; so however, that any such modification or annulment shall be without prejudice to the validity of anything previously done under that rule.

The Seeds (Amendment) Act, 1972 (No. 55 of 1972) (9th September, 1972)

An Act to amend the Seeds Act, 1966

BE it enacted by Parliament in the Twenty-third Year of the Republic of India as follows:-

Short Title and Commencement

1. (1) This Act may be called the Seeds (Amendment) Act, 1972

(2) It shall come into force on such date as the Central Government may, by notification in the Official Gazette, appoint.

Amendment of Section 2 of 1966

2. In section 2 of the Seeds Act, 1966 (hereinafter referred to as the principal Act), in clause (11), after sub-clause (iii), the following sub-clause shall be inserted, namely:-

"(iv) jute seeds,"

Insertion of New Sections 8A to 8E

3. After section 8 of the principal Act, the following sections shall be inserted, namely:-

The Central Seed Certification Board

"8A.(1)The Central Government shall, by notification in the Official Gazette, establish a Central Seed Certification Board (hereinafter referred to as the Board) to advise the Central Government and the State Governments on all matters relating to certification and to co-ordinate the functioning of the agencies established under section 8.

(2) The Board shall consist of the following members, namely:-

(i) a Chairman, to be nominated by the Central Government;

(ii) four members, to be nominated by the Central Government from out of the persons employed by the State Governments as Directors of Agriculture;

(iii) three members, to be nominated by the Central Government from out of the persons employed by the Agricultural Universities as Directors of Research;

(iv) thirteen persons, to be nominated by the Central Government to represent such interests as that Government thinks fit, of whom not less than four persons shall be representatives of seed producers or tradesmen.

(3) A member of the Board shall, unless his seat becomes vacant earlier by resignation or otherwise, be entitled to hold office for two years from the date of his nomination:

Provided that a person nominated under clause (ii) or clause (iii) of sub-section (2) shall hold office only for so long as he holds the appointment by virtue of which his nomination was made. Other Committees

8B. The Board may appoint as many Committees as it deems fit consisting wholly of the members of the Board or wholly of other persons or partly of members of the Board and partly of other persons as it thinks fit to exercise such powers and perform such duties as may be delegated to them, subject to such conditions as it may think fit, by the Board.

Proceedings of Board or Committee not to be Invalid by Reason of any Vacancy therein

8C. No proceeding of the Board or any Committee thereof shall become invalid merely by reason of the existence of any vacancy therein or any defect in the constitution thereof.

Procedure for Board

8D. The Board may, subject to the previous approval of the Central Government, make bye-laws for the purpose of regulating its own procedure and the procedure of any Committee thereof and the conduct of all business to be transacted by it or such Committee.

Secretary and other Officers

8E. The Central Government shall-

(i) appoint a person to be the Secretary of the Board, and

(ii) provide the Board with such technical and other staff as the Central Government considers necessary."

Amendment of Section 9

4. In section 9 of the principal Act,-

(i) in sub-section (3), for the words, brackets, letter and figure "minimum limits of germination and purity specified for that seed under clause (a) of section 6", the words "prescribed standards" shall be substituted;

(ii) to sub-section (3), the following proviso shall be added, namely:-

"Provided that such standards shall not be lower than the minimum limits of germination and purity specified for that seed under clause (a) of section 6."

Amendment of Section 25

5. In section 25 of the principal Act,-

(a) in sub-section (2), after clause (f), the following clause shall be inserted, namely:-

(ff) the standards to which seeds should conform,;

(b) in sub-section (3), for the words "in two successive sessions, and if, before the expiry of the session in which it is so laid or the session immediately following", the words "in two or more successive sessions, and if, before the expiry of the session immediately following the session or the successive sessions aforesaid" shall be substituted.

The Seeds Rules, 1968 under Seed Act, 1966 (Act No. 54 of 1966)

Part I - Preliminary

1. Short title. - These rules may be called the Seeds Rules, 1968.

2. Definitions. - In these rules, unless the context otherwise requires,

(a) "Act" means the Seeds Act, 1966 (54 of 1966);

(b) "advertisement" means all representations other than those on the label, disseminated in any manner or by any means relating to seed for the purposes of the Act;

(c) "certification sample" means a sample of seed drawn by a certification agency or by a duly authorised representative of a certification agency established under section 8 or recognized under section 18 of the Act;

(d) "certification tag" means a tag or label of certain design to be specified by the certification agency and shall constitute the certificate granted by the certification agency;

(e) "certified seed" means seed that fulfils all requirements for certification provided by the Act and these rules and to the container of which the certification tag is attached;

(f) "certified seed producer" means a person who grow or distributes certified seed in accordance with the procedure and standards of the certification agency;

(g) "complete record" means the information which relates to the origin, variety, kind, germination and purity of seed of any notified kind or variety offered for sale, sold or otherwise supplied;

(h) "form" means a form appended to these rules;

(i) "origin" means the State, Union Territory or foreign country where the seed is grown and in case seeds of different origin are blended the label shall show the percentage of seed of each origin;

(j) "processing" means cleaning, drying, treating, grading and other operations which would change the purity and germination of the seed and thus requiring re-testing to determine the quality of the seed, but does not include operations such as packaging and labelling;

(k) "section" means a section of the Act;

(l) "service sample" means a sample submitted to the Central Seed Laboratory or to a State Seed Laboratory for testing, the results to be used as information for seeding, selling or labelling purposes;

(m) "treated" means that the seed has been subjected to an application of a substance or process in such a manner as to reduce, control or repel certain disease organisms, insects, or any other pests attacking such seeds or seedlings growing therefrom and for other purposes.

Part II - Central Seed Committee

3. Functions of the Central Seed Committee. - In addition to the functions entrusted to the Committee by the Act, the Committee shall,-

(a) recommend the rate of fees to be levied for analysis of samples by the Central and State Seed Testing Laboratories and for certification by the certification agencies;

(b) advise the Central or State Governments on the suitability of seed testing laboratories;

(c) send its recommendations and other concerning records to the Central Government;

(d) recommend the procedure and standards for certification, tests and analysis of seeds; and

(e) carry out such other functions as are supplemental, incidental or consequential to any of the functions conferred by the Act or these rules.

4. *Travelling and Daily Allowances Payable to Members of the Committee and its sub-Committees.* - The members

of the committee and its sub-committees shall be entitled to draw travelling and daily allowances as specified below when they are called upon to attend a meeting of the committee or a sub-committee thereof:

(a) An official member of the committee or its sub-committees shall be entitled to draw travelling and daily allowances in accordance with the rules of the Government under which he is for the time being employed and from the same source from which his pay and allowances are drawn.

(b) A non-official member shall be allowed travelling and daily allowances in accordance with the general orders issued in this behalf by the Central Government from time to time.

Part III - Central Seed Laboratory

5. *Functions.* - In addition to the functions entrusted to the Central Seed Laboratory by the Act, the Laboratory shall carry out the following functions, namely:-

(a) initiate testing programmes in collaboration with the State Seed Laboratories designed to promote uniformity in test results between all seed laboratories in India.

(b) collect data continually on the quality of seeds found in the market and make this data available to the Committee; and

(c) carry out such other functions as may be assigned to it by the Central Government from time to time.

Part IV - Seed Certification Agency

6. *Functions of the Certification Agency.* - In addition to the functions entrusted to the certification agency by the Act, the Agency shall-

(a) certify seeds of any notified kinds or varieties;

(b) outline the procedure for submission of applications and for growing, harvesting, processing, storage and labellilng of seeds intended for certification till the end to ensure that seed lots finally approved for certification are true to variety and meet prescribed standards for certification under the Act or these rules;

(c) maintain a list of recognised breeders of seeds;

(d) verify, upon receipt of an application for certification that the variety is eligible for certification, that the seed source used for planting was authenticated and the record of purchase is in accordance with these rules and the fees have been paid;

(e) take sample and inspect seed lots produced under the procedure laid down by the certification agency and have such samples tested to ensure that the seed conforms to the prescribed standards of certification;

(f) inspect seed processing plants to see that the admixtures of other kinds and varieties are not introduced;

(g) ensure that action at all stages, e.g. field inspection, seed processing plant inspection, analysis of samples taken and issue of certificates (including tags, marks, labels and seals) is taken expeditiously;

(h) carry out educational programmes designed to promote the use of certified seed including a publication listing certified seed growers and sources of certified seed;

(i) grant certificates (including tags labels, seals etc.) in accordance with the provisions of the Act and these rules;

(j) maintain such records as may be necessary to verify that seed plants for the production of certified seed were eligible for such planting under these rules;

(k) inspect fields to ensure that the minimum standards for isolation, roguing (where applicable) use of male sterility (where applicable) and similar factors are maintained at all times, as well as ensure that seedborne diseases are not present in the field to a greater extent than those provided in the standards for certification.

Part V - Marking or Labelling

7. *Responsibility for Marking or Labelling.*—When seed of a notified kind or variety is offered for sale under section 7, each container shall be marked or labelled in the manner hereinafter specified. The person whose name appears on the mark or label shall be responsible for the accuracy of the information required to appear on the mark or label so long as seed is contained in the unopened original container:

Provided, however, that such person shall not be responsible for the accuracy of the statement appearing on the mark or label if the seed is removed from the original unopened container, or he shall not be responsible for the accuracy of the germination statement beyond the date of validity indicated on the mark or label.

8. Contents of the mark or label. - There shall be specified on every mark or label-

(i) particulars, as specified by the Central Government under clause (b) of section 6 of the Act;

(ii) a correct statement of the net content in terms of weight and expressed in metric system;

(iii) date of testing;

(iv) if the seed in container has been treated-

(a) a statement indicating that the seed has been treated;

(b) the commonly accepted chemical or abbreviated chemical (generic) name of the applied substance; and

(c) if the substance of the chemical used for treatment, and present with the seed is harmful to human beings or other vertebrate animals, a caution statement such as "Do not use for food, feed or oil purposes". The caution for mercurials and similarly toxic substance shall be the word "Poison" which shall be in type size, prominently displayed on the label in red:

(v) the name and address of the person who offers for sale, sells or otherwise supplies the seed and who is responsible for its quality;

(vi) the name of the seed as notified under section 5 of the Act.

9. *Manner of marking or labelling the container under clause (C) of section 7 and clause (B) of section 17*—

(1) The mark or label containing the particulars of the seed as specified under clause (b) of section 6 shall appear on each container of seed or on a tag or mark or label attached to the container in a conspicuous place on the innermost container in which the seed is packed and on every other covering in which that container is packed and shall be legible.

(2) Any transparent cover or any wrapper, case or other covering used solely for the purpose of packing of transport or delivery need not be marked or labelled.

(3) Where by a provision of these rules, any particulars are required to be displayed on a label on the container, such particulars may, instead of being displayed on a label be etched, painted or otherwise indelibly marked on the container.

10. *Mark or Label not to contain false or misleading statement.* - The mark or label shall not contain any statement, claim, design, device, fancy name or abbreviation which is false or misleading in any particular concerning the seed contained in the container.

11. *Mark or label not to contain reference to the Act or Rules contradictory to required particulars.* - The mark or label shall not contain any reference to the Act, or any of these, rules or any comment on, or reference to, or explanation of any particulars or declaration required by the Act or any of these rules which directly or by implication contradicts, qualifies or modifies such particulars or declaration.

12. *Denial of Responsibility for mark or label content prohibited.* - Nothing shall appear on the mark or label or in any advertisement pertaining to any seed of any notified kind or variety which shall deny responsibility for the statement required by or under the Act to appear on such mark, label or advertisement.

Part VI - Requirements

13. *Requirements to be complied with by a person carrying on the Business referred to in Section 7.* -

(1) No person shall sell, keep for sale, offer to sell, barter or otherwise supply any seed of any notified kind or variety, after the date recorded on the container, mark or label as the date upto which the seed may be expected to retain the germination not less than that prescribed under clause (a) of section 6 of the Act.

(2) No person shall after, obliterate or deface any mark or label attached to the container of any seed.

(3) Every person selling, keeping for sale, offering to sell, bartering or otherwise supplying any seed of notified kind or variety under section 7, shall keep over a period of three years a complete record of each lot of seed sold except that any seed sample may be discarded one year after the entire lot represented by such sample has been disposed of. The sample of seed kept as part of the complete record shall be as large as the size notified in the official Gazette. This sample, if required to be tested, shall be tested only for determining the purity.

(14) *Classes and sources of certified seed.* - (1) There shall be three classes of certified seed, namely, foundations, registered and certified and each class shall meet the following standards for that class:-

(a) Foundation seed shall be the progeny of breeders' seed, or be produced from foundation seed which can be clearly traced to breeder's seed. Production shall be supervised and approved by a seed certification agency and be so handled as to maintain specific genetic purity and identify and shall be required to meet certification standards for the crop being certified.

(b) Registered seed shall be the progeny of foundation seed that is so handled as to maintain its genetic identity and purity according to standard specified for the particular crop being certified.

(c) Certified seed shall be the progeny of registered or foundation seed that is so handled to maintain genetic identity and purity according to standards specified for the particular crop being certified. (2) At the discretion of the certification agency (when considered necessary to maintain adequate seed supplies) certified seed may be the progeny of certified seed provided this reproduction may not exceed three generations and provided further that it is determined by the seed certification agency, that the genetic purity will not be significantly altered.

Part VII - Certification of Seeds

15. Application for the Grant of a Certificate. - Every

application for the grant of a certificate under sub-section (1) of section 9 shall be made in Form I in accordance with the procedure outlined by the certification agency for submission of applications and contain the following particulars, namely:-

(a) the name, profession, and place of residence of the applicant;

(b) the name of the seed to be certified; its notified kind or variety;

(c) class of the seed;

(d) source of the seed;

(e) limits of germination and purity of the seed

;(f) mark or label of the seed.

16. *Fees*—Every application under sub-section (1) of section 9 shall be accompanied by a fee of Rs. 25 in cash.

17. *Certificate*—Every certificate granted under sub-section (3) of section 9 shall be in Form II and shall be granted by the certification agency, after making enquiries and satisfying itself in accordance with the provisions of the said sub-section on the following conditions, for the period to be specified by the certification agency, namely:-

(i) The person to whom the certificate is granted under sub-section (3) of section 9 shall attach a certification tag to every container of the certified seed and shall follow the provisions in respect of marking or labelling provided by or under the Act.

(ii) The certification tag shall contain the following particulars, namely:-

(a) name and address of the certification agency;

(b) kind and variety of the seed;

(c) lot number or other mark of the seed;

(d) name and address of the certified seed producer;

(e) date of issue of the certificate and of its validity;

(f) an appropriate sign to designate certified seed;

(g) an appropriate word denoting the class designation of the seed.

(iii) The colour of the certification tag shall be white for foundation seed, purple for registered seed and blue for certified seed.

(iv) The container of the certified seed shall carry a seal of such material and in such form as the certification agency may determine and no container carrying a certification tag shall be sold by the person if the tag or seal has either been tampered with or removed.

(v) The certification tag on the container shall specify-

(a) the period during which the seed shall be used for sowing or planting;

(b) that the use of seed after the expiry of the validity period by any person is entirely at his risk and the holder of the certificate shall not be responsible for any damage to the buyer of the seed;

(c) that no one should purchase the seed if the seal or the certification tag has been tampered with.

(vi) The holder of the certificate shall keep record of the details of each lot of the seed which is issued for sale in such form as to be available for inspection and to be easily identified by reference to the number of the lot as shown in the certification tag of each container and such records shall be retained in the case of a seed for which expiry date is fixed for a period of two years from the expiry of such date.

(vii) The holder of the certificate shall allow any Seed Inspector, authorised in writing by the certification agency in that behalf, to enter with or without prior notice the premises where the seeds are grown processed and sold and to inspect premises, plant and the process of processing at all reasonable hours.

(viii) The holder of the certificate shall allow the Seed Inspector, authorised in writing by the certification agency, to inspect all registers and records maintained under these rules and to take samples of the seeds and shall supply to the Seed Inspector such information as he may require for the purposes of ascertaining whether the conditions subject to which the certificate has been granted, have been complied with.

(ix) The holder of the certificate shall on request furnish to the certification agency from every lot of the seed or from such lot or lots as the said agency may from time to time specify, a sample of such quantity as the agency may consider adequate for any examination required to be made.

(x) If the certification agency so directs, the holder of the certificate shall not sell or offer for sale any lot in respect of which a sample is furnished under the preceding clause until the agency authorises the sale of such lot.

(xi) The holder of the certificate shall on being directed by the certification agency that any part of a lot has been found by the said agency not to conform to prescribed standards of quality or purity specified by or under the Act, withdraw the remainder of that lot from sale and so far as may, in the particular circumstances of the case, be practicable, recall all issues already made from that lot.

(xii) The holder of the certificate shall comply with the provisions of the Act and these rules and with the directions given after not less than one month's notice by the certification agency to such holder.

Part VIII - Appeals

18. *The form and manner in which and the fee on payment of which the appeal may be referred.* -

(1) Every memorandum of appeal under sub-section (1) of section 11 shall be in writing and shall be accompanied by a copy of the decision of the certification agency against which it has been preferred and shall set forth concisely and under distinct heads the grounds of objection to such decision without any argument, or narrative.

(2) Every such memorandum of appeal shall be accompanied by a treasury receipt for a sum of Rs. 100/-/

(3) Every such memorandum of appeal may be presented either in person or through an agent

duly authorised in writing in this behalf by the appellant or may be sent by the registered post.

19. Procedure to be followed by the Appellate Authority. - In deciding appeals under the Act the appellate authority shall exercise all the powers which a Court has and shall follow the same procedure which a Court follows in deciding appeals from the decree or order of an original Court under the Code of Civil Procedure, 1908 (5 of 1908)

Part IX - Seed Analysts and Seed Inspectors

20. Qualifications of Seed Analyst. - A person shall not be qualified for appointment as Seed Analyst unless he-

    (i) possesses a Master's or equivalent degree in Agriculture or Agronomy or Botany or Horticulture of a University recognised for this purpose by the Government and has had not less than one year's experience in seed technology; or

    (ii) possesses a Bachelor's degree in Agriculture or Botany of a University recognised for this purpose by the Government and has had not less than three years' experience in seed technology.

21. *Duties of a Seed Analyst.* - On receipt of a sample for analysis the Seed Analyst shall first ascertain that the mark and the seal or fastening as provided in clause (b) of sub-section

    (1) of section 15 are intact and shall note the condition of the seals thereon.

(2) The Seed Analyst shall analyse the samples according to the provisions of the Act and these rules.

(3) The Seed Analyst shall deliver the copy of the report of the result of the analysis to the persons specified in sub-section (1) of section 16.

(4) The Seed Analyst shall from time to time forward to the State Government the reports giving the result of analytical work done by him.

22. *Qualifications of Seed Inspectors.* - A person shall not be qualified for appointment as Seed Inspector unless he is a graduate in Agriculture of a University recognised for the purpose by the Government and has had not less than one years experience in seed production, or seed development or seed analysis or testing in a seed testing laboratory.

(a) inspect as frequently as may be required by certification agency all places used for growing, storage or sale of any seed of any notified kind or variety;

(b) satisfy himself that the conditions of the certificates are being observed;

(c) procure and send for analysis, if necessary, samples of any seeds, which he has reason to suspect are being produced stocked or sold or exhibited for sale in contravention of the provisions of the Act or these rules;

(d) investigate any complaint, which may be made to him in writing in respect of any contravention of the provisions of the Act or these rules;

(e) maintain a record of all inspections made and action taken by him in the performance of his duties including the taking of samples and the seizure of stocks and submit copies of such record to the Director of Agriculture or the certification agency as may be directed in this behalf;

(f) when so authorised by the State Government detain imported containers which he has reason to suspect contain seeds, import of which is prohibited except and in accordance with the provisions of the Act and these rules;

(g) institute prosecutions in respect of breaches of the Act and these rules; and

(h) perform such other duties as may be entrusted to him by the competent authority.

Part X - Sealing, Fastening, Despatch and Analysis of Samples

24. *Manner of taking Samples.* - Samples of any seed of any notified kind or variety for the purpose of analysis shall be taken in a clean dry container which shall be closed sufficiently tight to prevent leakage and entrance of moisture and shall be carefully sealed.

25. *Containers to be labelled and addressed.* - All containers containing samples for analysis shall be properly labelled and the parcels shall be properly addressed. The label on any sample of seed sent for analysis shall bear-

(a) serial number;

(b) name of the sender with official designation, if any;

(c) name of the person from whom the sample has been taken;

(d) date and place of taking the sample;

(e) kind or variety of the seed for analysis;

(f) nature and quantity of preservative, if any, added to the sample;

26. *Manner of Packing, Fastening and Sealing the Samples.* - All samples of seeds sent for analysis shall be packed, fastened and sealed in the following manner:

(a) The stopper shall first be securely fastened so as to prevent leakage of the containers in transit.

(b) The container shall then be completely wrapped in fairly strong thick paper. The ends of the paper shall be neatly folded in and affixed by means of gum or other adhesive.

(c) The paper cover shall be further secured by means of strong twine or thread both above and across the container, and the twine or thread shall then be fastened on the paper cover by means of sealing wax on which there shall be at least four distinct and clear impressions of the seal of the sender, of which one shall be at the top of the packet, one at the bottom and the other two on the body of the packet. The knots of the twine or thread shall be covered by means of sealing wax bearing the impression of the seal of the sender.

27. *Form of Order.* - The order to be given in writing by the Seed Inspector under clause (c) of sub-section (1) of section 14 shall be in Form III.

28. *Form of Receipt for Records.* - When a Seed Inspector seizes any record, register, document or any other material object under clause (d) of sub-section (1) of section 14, he shall issue a receipt in Form IV to the person concerned.

29. *Samples how to be sent to the Seed Analyst.* - The container of sample for analysis shall be sent to the Seed Analyst by registered post or by hand in a sealed packed enclosed together with a memorandum in Form V in an outer cover addressed to the Seed Analyst.

30. *Memorandum and Impression of seal to be sent separately.* - A copy of the memorandum and a specimen impression of the seal used to seal the packet shall be sent to the Seed Analyst separately by régistered post or delivered to him or to any person authorised by him.

31. *Addition of Preservatives to Samples.* - Any person taking a sample of seed for the purpose of analysis under the Act may add a preservative as may be specified from time to time to the sample for the purpose of maintaining it in a condition suitable for analysis.

32. *Nature and Quantity of the Preservative to be noted on the Label.* - Whenever any preservative is added to a sample, the nature and quantity of the preservative added shall be clearly noted on the label to be affixed to the container.

33. *Analysis of the Sample.* - On receipt of the packet, it shall be opened either by the Seed Analyst or by an officer authorised in writing in that behalf by the Seed Analyst, who shall record the condition of the seal on the packet. Analysis of the sample shall be carried out at the State Seed Laboratory in

accordance with the procedure laid down by the Central Government.

34. *Form of Notice.* - The notice to be given under clause (a) of sub-section (1) of section 15 to the person from whom the Seed Inspector intends to take sample shall be in Form VI.

35. *Form of Report.* - The report of the result of the analysis under sub-section (1) or sub-section (2) of section 16 shall be delivered or sent in Form VII.

36. *Fees.* - The fees payable in respect of the report from the Central Seed Laboratory under sub-section (2) of section 16 shall be Rs. 10/- per sample of the seed analysed.

37. *Retaining of the Sample.* - The sample of any seed shall, under clause (c) of sub-section (2) of section 15, be retained under a cool, dry environment to eliminate the loss of viability and insect proof or rat proof container. The containers shall be dusted with suitable insecticides and the storage room fumigated to avoid infestation of samples by insects. The sample shall be packed in good quality containers of uniform shape and size before storage.

Part XI - Miscellaneous

38. *Records.* - A person carrying on the business referred to in section 7 shall maintain the following records, namely:-

    (a) stock record of seed;

    (b) record of the sale of seeds;

39. *Form of Memorandum.* - The memorandum to be prepared under subsection (4) of section 14 shall be in Form VIII.

2

The Seeds Rules, 1968

Part I - Preliminary

1. *Short title.* – These rules may be called the Seeds Rules, 1968.
2. *Definitions.* – In these rules, unless the context otherwise requires,-
   (a) "Act" means the Seeds Act, 1966 (54 of 1966);
   (b) "advertisement" means all representations other than those on the label, disseminated in any manner or by any means relating to seed for the purposes of the Act;
   (c) "certification sample" means a sample of seed drawn by a certification agency or by a duly authorised representative of a certification agency established under section 8 or recognized under section 18 of the Act;
   (d) "certification tag" means a tag or label of certain design to be specified by the certification agency and shall constitute the certificate granted by the certification agency;
   (e) "certified seed" means seed that fulfils all requirements for certification provided by the

Act and these rules and to the container of which the certification tag is attached;

(f) "certified seed producer" means a person who grow or distributes certified seed in accordance with the procedure and standards of the certification agency;

(g) "complete record" means the information which relates to the origin, variety, kind, germination and purity of seed of any notified kind or variety offered for sale, sold or otherwise supplied;

(h) "form" means a form appended to these rules;

(i) "origin" means the State, Union Territory or foreign country where the seed is grown and in case seeds of different origin are blended the label shall show the percentage of seed of each origin;

(j) "processing" means cleaning, drying, treating, grading and other operations which would change the purity and germination of the seed and thus requiring re-testing to determine the quality of the seed, but does not include operations such as packaging and labelling;

(k) "section" means a section of the Act;

(l) "service sample" means a sample submitted to the Central Seed Laboratory or to a State Seed Laboratory for testing, the results to be used as information for seeding, selling or labelling purposes;

(m) "treated" means that the seed has been subjected to an application of a substance or process in such a manner as to reduce, control or repel certain disease organisms, insects, or any other pests attacking such seeds or seedlings growing therefrom and for other purposes.

PART II – Central Seed Committee

3. *Functions of the Central Seed Committee.* – In addition to the functions entrusted to the Committee by the Act, the Committee shall,-

(a) recommend the rate of fees to be levied for analysis of samples by the Central and State Seed Testing Laboratories and for certification by the certification agencies;

(b) advise the Central or State Governments on the suitability of seed testing laboratories;

(c) send its recommendations and other concerning records to the Central Government;

(d) recommend the procedure and standards for certification, tests and analysis of seeds; and

(e) carry out such other functions as are supplemental, incidental or consequential to any of the functions conferred by the Act or these rules.

4. *Travelling and Daily Allowances Payable to Members of the Committee and its sub-Committees.* – The members of the committee and its sub-committees shall be entitled to draw travelling and daily allowances as specified below when they are called upon to attend a meeting of the committee or a sub-committee thereof:

(a) An official member of the committee or its sub-committees shall be entitled to draw travelling and daily allowances in accordance with the rules of the

Government under which he is for the time being employed and from the same source from which his pay and allowances are drawn.

(b) A non-official member shall be allowed travelling and daily allowances in accordance with the general orders issued in this behalf by the Central Government from time to time.

PART III – Central Seed Laboratory

5. *Functions.* – In addition to the functions entrusted to the Central Seed Laboratory by the Act, the Laboratory shall carry out the following functions, namely:-

(a) initiate testing programmes in collaboration with the State Seed Laboratories designed to promote uniformity in test results between all seed laboratories in India.

(b) collect data continually on the quality of seeds found in the market and make this data available to the Committee; and

(c) carry out such other functions as may be assigned to it by the Central Government from time to time.

PART IV – Seed Certification Agency

6. *Functions of the Certification Agency.* – In addition to the functions entrusted to the certification agency by the Act, the Agency shall-

(a) certify seeds of any notified kinds or varieties;

(b) outline the procedure for submission of applications and for growing, harvesting, processing, storage and labellilng of seeds intended for certification till the end to ensure that seed lots finally approved for certification are true to variety and meet prescribed standards for certification under the Act or these rules;

(c) maintain a list of recognised breeders of seeds;

(d) verify, upon receipt of an application for certification that the variety is eligible for certification, that the seed source used for planting was authenticated and the record of purchase is in accordance with these rules and the fees have been paid;

(e) take sample and inspect seed lots produced under the procedure laid down by the certification agency and have such samples tested to ensure that the seed conforms to the prescribed standards of certification;

(f) inspect seed processing plants to see that the admixtures of other kinds and varieties are not introduced;

(g) ensure that action at all stages, e.g. field inspection, seed processing plant inspection, analysis of samples taken and issue of certificates (including tags, marks, labels and seals) is taken expeditiously;

(h) carry out educational programmes designed to promote the use of certified seed including a publication listing certified seed growers and sources of certified seed;

(i) grant certificates (including tags labels, seals etc.) in accordance with the provisions of the Act and these rules;

(j) maintain such records as may be necessary to verify that seed plants for the production of certified seed were eligible for such planting under these rules;

(k) inspect fields to ensure that the minimum standards for isolation, roguing (where applicable) use of male sterility (where applicable) and similar factors are maintained at all times, as well as ensure that seedborne diseases are not present in the field to a greater extent than those provided in the standards for certification.

Part V – Marking or Labelling

7. *Responsibility for Marking or Labelling.* – When seed of a notified kind or variety is offered for sale under section 7, each container shall be marked or labelled in the manner hereinafter specified. The person whose name appears on the mark or label shall be responsible for the accuracy of the information required to appear on the mark or label so long as seed is contained in the unopened original container:

Provided, however, that such person shall not be responsible for the accuracy of the statement appearing on the mark or label if the seed is removed from the original unopened container, or he shall not be responsible for the accuracy of the germination statement beyond the date of validity indicated on the mark or label.

8. *Contents of the mark or label.* – There shall be specified on every mark or label-

(i) particulars, as specified by the Central Government under clause (b) of section 6 of the Act;

(ii) a correct statement of the net content in terms of weight and expressed in metric system;

(iii) date of testing;

(iv) if the seed in container has been treated-

(a) a statement indicating that the seed has been treated;

(b) the commonly accepted chemical or abbreviated chemical (generic) name of the applied substance; and

(c) if the substance of the chemical used for treatment, and present with the seed is harmful to human beings or other vertebrate animals, a caution statement such as "Do not use for food, feed or oil purposes". The caution for mercurials and similarly toxic substance shall be the word "Poison" which shall be in type size, prominently displayed on the label in red:

(v) the name and address of the person who offers for sale, sells or otherwise supplies the seed and who is responsible for its quality;

(vi) the name of the seed as notified under section 5 of the Act.

9. *Manner of marking or labelling the container under clause (C) of section 7 and clause (B) of section 17.* – (1) The mark or label containing the particulars of the seed as specified under clause (b) of section 6 shall appear on each container of seed or on a tag or mark or label attached to the container in a conspicuous place on the innermost container in which the seed is packed and on every other covering in which that container is packed and shall be legible.

(2) Any transparent cover or any wrapper, case or other covering used solely for the purpose of

packing of transport or delivery need not be marked or labelled.

(3) Where by a provision of these rules, any particulars are required to be displayed on a label on the container, such particulars may, instead of being displayed on a label be etched, painted or otherwise indelibly marked on the container.

10. *Mark or Label not to contain false or misleading statement.* – The mark or label shall not contain any statement, claim, design, device, fancy name or abbreviation which is false or misleading in any particular concerning the seed contained in the container.

11. *Mark or label not to contain reference to the Act or Rules* contradictory to required particulars. – The mark or label shall not contain any reference to the Act, or any of these, rules or any comment on, or reference to, or explanation of any particulars or declaration required by the Act or any of these rules which directly or by implication contradicts, qualifies or modifies such particulars or declaration.

12. *Denial of Responsibility for mark or label content prohibited.* – Nothing shall appear on the mark or label or in any advertisement pertaining to any seed of any notified kind or variety which shall deny responsibility for the statement required by or under the Act to appear on such mark, label or advertisement.

Part VI – Requirements

13. *Requirements to be complied with by a person carrying on the Business referred to in Section 7.* –

(1) No person shall sell, keep for sale, offer to sell, barter or otherwise supply any seed of any notified kind or variety, after the date recorded on the container, mark or label as the date upto which the seed may be expected to retain the germination not less than that prescribed under clause (a) of section 6 of the Act.

(2) No person shall after, obliterate or deface any mark or label attached to the container of any seed.

(3) Every person selling, keeping for sale, offering to sell, bartering or otherwise supplying any seed of notified kind or variety under section 7, shall keep over a period of three years a complete record of each lot of seed sold except that any seed sample may be discarded one year after the entire lot represented by such sample has been disposed of. The sample of seed kept as part of the complete record shall be as large as the size notified in the official Gazette. This sample, if required to be tested, shall be tested only for determining the purity.

(14) *Classes and sources of certified seed.* – (1) There shall be three classes of certified seed, namely, foundations, registered and certified and each class shall meet the following standards for that class:-

(a) Foundation seed shall be the progeny of breeders' seed, or be produced from foundation seed which can be clearly traced to breeder's seed. Production shall be supervised and approved by a seed certification agency and be so handled as to maintain specific genetic purity and identify and shall be required to meet certification standards for the crop being certified.

(b) Registered seed shall be the progeny of foundation seed that is so handled as to maintain its genetic identity and purity according to standard specified for the particular crop being certified.

(c) Certified seed shall be the progeny of registered or foundation seed that is so handled to maintain genetic identity and purity according to standards specified for the particular crop being certified.

(2) At the discretion of the certification agency (when considered necessary to maintain adequate seed supplies) certified seed may be the progeny of certified seed provided this reproduction may not exceed three generations and provided further that it is determined by the seed certification agency, that the genetic purity will not be significantly altered.

Part VII – Certification of Seeds

15. *Application for the Grant of a Certificate.* – Every application for the grant of a certificate under sub-section (1) of section 9 shall be made in Form I in accordance with the procedure outlined by the certification agency for submission of applications and contain the following particulars, namely:-

(a) the name, profession, and place of residence of the applicant;

(b) the name of the seed to be certified; its notified kind or variety;

(c) class of the seed;

(d) source of the seed;

(e) limits of germination and purity of the seed;

(f) mark or label of the seed.

16. *Fees.* – Every application under sub-section (1) of section 9 shall be accompanied by a fee of Rs. 25 in cash.

17. *Certificate.* – Every certificate granted under sub-section (3) of section 9 shall be in Form II and shall be granted by the certification agency, after making enquiries and satisfying itself in accordance with the provisions of the said sub-section on the following conditions, for the period to be specified by the certification agency, namely:-

(i) The person to whom the certificate is granted under sub-section (3) of section 9 shall attach a certification tag to every container of the certified seed and shall follow the provisions in respect of marking or labelling provided by or under the Act.

(ii) The certification tag shall contain the following particulars, namely:-

(a) name and address of the certification agency;

(b) kind and variety of the seed;

(c) lot number or other mark of the seed;

(d) name and address of the certified seed producer;

(e) date of issue of the certificate and of its validity;

(f) an appropriate sign to designate certified seed;

(g) an appropriate word denoting the class designation of the seed.

(iii) The colour of the certification tag shall be white for foundation seed, purple for registered seed and blue for certified seed.

(iv) The container of the certified seed shall carry a seal of such material and in such form as the certification agency may determine and no container carrying a certification tag shall be sold by the person if the tag or seal has either been tampered with or removed.

(v) The certification tag on the container shall specify-

(a) the period during which the seed shall be used for sowing or planting;

(b) that the use of seed after the expiry of the validity period by any person is entirely at his risk and the holder of the certificate shall not be responsible for any damage to the buyer of the seed;

(c) that no one should purchase the seed if the seal or the certification tag has been tampered with.

(vi) The holder of the certificate shall keep record of the details of each lot of the seed which is issued for sale in such form as to be available for inspection and to be easily identified by reference to the number of the lot as shown in the certification tag of each container and such records shall be retained in the case of a seed for which expiry date is fixed for a period of two years from the expiry of such date.

(vii) The holder of the certificate shall allow any Seed Inspector, authorised in writing by the certification agency in that behalf, to enter with or without prior notice the premises where the seeds are grown processed and sold and to inspect premises, plant and the process of processing at all reasonable hours.

(viii) The holder of the certificate shall allow the Seed Inspector, authorised in writing by the certification agency, to inspect all registers and records maintained under these rules and to take samples of the seeds and shall supply to the Seed Inspector such information as he may require for the purposes of ascertaining whether the conditions subject to which the certificate has been granted, have been complied with.

(ix) The holder of the certificate shall on request furnish to the certification agency from every lot of the seed or from such lot or lots as the said agency may from time to time specify, a sample of such quantity as the agency may consider adequate for any examination required to be made.

(x) If the certification agency so directs, the holder of the certificate shall not sell or offer for sale any lot in respect of which a sample is furnished under the preceding clause until the agency authorises the sale of such lot.

(xi) The holder of the certificate shall on being directed by the certification agency that any part of a lot has been found by the said agency not to conform to prescribed standards of quality or purity specified by or under the Act, withdraw the remainder of that lot from sale and so far as may, in the particular circumstances of the case, be practicable, recall all issues already made from that lot.

(xii) The holder of the certificate shall comply with the provisions of the Act and these rules and with the directions given after not less than one month's notice by the certification agency to such holder.

Part VIII – Appeals

18. *The form and manner in which and the fee on payment of which the appeal may be referred.* – (1) Every memorandum of appeal under sub-section (1) of section 11 shall be in writing and shall be accompanied by a copy of the decision of the certification agency against which it has been preferred and shall set forth concisely and under distinct heads the grounds of objection to such decision without any argument, or narrative.

(2) Every such memorandum of appeal shall be accompanied by a treasury receipt for a sum of Rs. 100/-/

(3) Every such memorandum of appeal may be presented either in person or through an agent duly authorised in writing in this behalf by the appellant or may be sent by the registered post.

19. *Procedure to be followed by the Appellate Authority.* – In deciding appeals under the Act the appellate authority shall exercise all the powers which a Court has and shall follow the same procedure which a Court follows in deciding appeals from the decree or order of an original Court under the Code of Civil Procedure, 1908 (5 of 1908)

Part IX – Seed Analysts and Seed Inspectors

20. *Qualifications of Seed Analyst.* – A person shall not be qualified for appointment as Seed Analyst unless he-

(i) possesses a Master's or equivalent degree in Agriculture or Agronomy or Botany or Horticulture of a University recognised for this purpose by the Government and has had not less than one year's experience in seed technology; or

(ii) possesses a Bachelor's degree in Agriculture or Botany of a University recognised for this purpose by the Government and has had not less than three years' experience in seed technology.

21. *Duties of a Seed Analyst.* – On receipt of a sample for analysis the Seed Analyst shall first ascertain that the mark and the seal or fastening as provided in clause (b) of sub-section (1) of section 15 are intact and shall note the condition of the seals thereon.

(2) The Seed Analyst shall analyse the samples according to the provisions of the Act and these rules.

(3) The Seed Analyst shall deliver the copy of the report of the result of the analysis to the persons specified in sub-section (1) of section 16.

(4) The Seed Analyst shall from time to time forward to the State Government the reports giving the result of analytical work done by him.

22. *Qualifications of Seed Inspectors.* – A person shall not be qualified for appointment as Seed Inspector

unless he is a graduate in Agriculture of a University recognised for the purpose by the Government and has had not less than one years experience in seed production, or seed development or seed analysis or testing in a seed testing laboratory.

(a) inspect as frequently as may be required by certification agency all places used for growing, storage or sale of any seed of any notified kind or variety;

(b) satisfy himself that the conditions of the certificates are being observed;

(c) procure and send for analysis, if necessary, samples of any seeds, which he has reason to suspect are being produced stocked or sold or exhibited for sale in contravention of the provisions of the Act or these rules;

(d) investigate any complaint, which may be made to him in writing in respect of any contravention of the provisions of the Act or these rules;

(e) maintain a record of all inspections made and action taken by him in the performance of his duties including the taking of samples and the seizure of stocks and submit copies of such record to the Director of Agriculture or the certification agency as may be directed in this behalf;

(f) when so authorised by the State Government detain imported containers which he has reason to suspect contain seeds, import of which is prohibited except and in accordance with the provisions of the Act and these rules;

(g) institute prosecutions in respect of breaches of the Act and these rules; and

(h) perform such other duties as may be entrusted to him by the competent authority.

Part X – Sealing, Fastening, Despatch and Analysis of Samples

24. *Manner of taking Samples.* – Samples of any seed of any notified kind or variety for the purpose of analysis shall be taken in a clean dry container which shall be closed sufficiently tight to prevent leakage and entrance of moisture and shall be carefully sealed.

25. *Containers to be labelled and addressed.* – All containers containing samples for analysis shall be properly labelled and the parcels shall be properly addressed. The label on any sample of seed sent for analysis shall bear-

(a) serial number;

(b) name of the sender with official designation, if any;

(c) name of the person from whom the sample has been taken;

(d) date and place of taking the sample;

(e) kind or variety of the seed for analysis;

(f) nature and quantity of preservative, if any, added to the sample;

26. *Manner of Packing, Fastening and Sealing the Samples.* – All samples of seeds sent for analysis shall be packed, fastened and sealed in the following manner:

(a) The stopper shall first be securely fastened so as to prevent leakage of the containers in transit.

(b) The container shall then be completely wrapped in fairly strong thick paper. The ends of the paper shall be neatly folded in and affixed by means of gum or other adhesive.

(c) The paper cover shall be further secured by means of strong twine or thread both above and across the container, and the twine or thread shall then be fastened on the paper cover by means of sealing wax on which there shall be at least four distinct and clear impressions of the seal of the sender, of which one shall be at the top of the packet, one at the bottom and the other two on the body of the packet. The knots of the twine or thread shall be covered by means of sealing wax bearing the impression of the seal of the sender.

27. *Form of Order.* – The order to be given in writing by the Seed Inspector under clause (c) of sub-section (1) of section 14 shall be in Form III.

28. *Form of Receipt for Records.* – When a Seed Inspector seizes any record, register, document or any other material object under clause (d) of sub-section (1) of section 14, he shall issue a receipt in Form IV to the person concerned.

29. *Samples how to be sent to the Seed Analyst.* – The container of sample for analysis shall be sent to the Seed Analyst by registered post or by hand in a sealed packed enclosed together with a memorandum in Form V in an outer cover addressed to the Seed Analyst.

30. *Memorandum and Impression of seal to be sent separately.* – A copy of the memorandum and a specimen impression of the seal used to seal the packet shall be sent to the Seed Analyst separately by registered post or delivered to him or to any person authorised by him.

31. *Addition of Preservatives to Samples.* – Any person taking a sample of seed for the purpose of analysis under the Act may add a preservative as may be specified from time to time to the sample for the purpose of maintaining it in a condition suitable for analysis.

32. N*ature and Quantity of the Preservative to be noted on the Label.* – Whenever any preservative is added to a sample, the nature and quantity of the preservative added shall be clearly noted on the label to be affixed to the container.

33. *Analysis of the Sample.* – On receipt of the packet, it shall be opened either by the Seed Analyst or by an officer authorised in writing in that behalf by the Seed Analyst, who shall record the condition of the seal on the packet. Analysis of the sample shall be carried out at the State Seed Laboratory in accordance with the procedure laid down by the Central Government.

34. *Form of Notice.* – The notice to be given under clause (a) of sub-section (1) of section 15 to the person from whom the Seed Inspector intends to take sample shall be in Form VI.

35. *Form of Report.* – The report of the result of the analysis under sub-section (1) or sub-section (2) of section 16 shall be delivered or sent in Form VII.

36. *Fees.* – The fees payable in respect of the report from the Central Seed Laboratory under sub-section (2) of section 16 shall be Rs. 10/- per sample of the seed analysed.

37. *Retaining of the Sample.* – The sample of any seed shall, under clause (c) of sub-section (2) of section 15, be retained under a cool, dry environment to eliminate the loss of viability and insect proof or rat proof container. The containers shall be dusted with suitable insecticides and the storage room fumigated to avoid infestation of samples by insects. The sample shall be packed in good quality containers of uniform shape and size before storage.

Part XI - Miscellaneous

38. *Records.* – A person carrying on the business referred to in section 7 shall maintain the following records, namely:-

 (a) stock record of seed;

 (b) record of the sale of seeds;

39. *Form of Memorandum.* – The memorandum to be prepared under subsection (4) of section 14 shall be in Form VIII.

3

Seed (Control) Order, 1983 under Essential Commodities Act, 1955 (10 of 1955)

The Seeds (Control) Order, 1983

New Delhi, dated the 30th Dec., 1983

Order

GSR 932 (E) - In exercise of the powers conferred by section 3 of the Essential Commodities Act, 1955 (10 of 1955), the Central Government hereby makes the following order, namely:-

Preliminary

1. *Short title and extent:*

   (i) This Order may be called the Seeds (Control) Order, 1983.

   (ii) It extends to the whole of India.

   (iii) It shall come into force on the 30th December, 1983.

2. *Definitions*

In this Order, unless the context otherwise requires,

(a) "Act" means the Essential Commodities Act, 1955 (10 of 1955).

(b) "Controller" means a person appointed as Controller of Seeds by the Central Government and includes any person empowered by the Central Government to exercise all or any functions of the Controller under this Order;

(c) "Dealer" means a person carrying on the business of selling, exporting or importing seeds, and includes an agent of a dealer;

(d) "Export" means to take or cause to be taken out from any place in India to a place outside India;

(e) "Form" means a form appended to this Order;

(f) "Import" means to bring or cause to be brought to any place in India from outside India;

(g) "Inspector" means an inspector of seeds appointed under clause 12;

(h) "Registering authority" means a licensing authority appointed under clause 11;

(i) "Seeds" means the seeds as defined in the Seeds Act, 1966 (54 of 1966).

(j) "State Government" in relation to a Union Territory means the Administrator thereof by whatever designation known.

Dealer in Seeds to be Licensed

3. Dealer to obtain licence :

(1) No person shall carry on the business of selling, exporting or importing seeds at any place except under and in accordance with the terms and conditions of licence granted to him under this order.

(2) Notwithstanding anything contained in sub-clause (1), the State Government may, by notification in the Official Gazette, exempt from the provisions of that sub-clause such class of dealers in such areas and subject to such conditions as may be specified in the notification.

4. Application for licence :

Every person desiring to obtain a licence for selling, exporting or importing seeds shall make an application in duplicate in Form 'A' together with a fee of rupees fifty for licence to licensing authority.

5. Grant and refusal of licence :

(1) The licensing authority may, after making such enquiry as it thinks fit, grant a licence in Form 'B' to any person who applies for it under clause 4:

Provided that a licence shall not be issued to a person-

(a) whose earlier licence granted under this Order is under suspension, during the period of such suspension;

(b) whose earlier licence granted under this Order has been cancelled, within a period of one year from the date of such cancellation.

(c) who has been convicted under the Essential Commodities Act, 1955 (10 of 1955) or any order issued thereunder within three years preceding the date of application.

(2) When the licensing authority refuses to grant licence to a person who applies for it under clause 4, he shall record his reasons for doing so.

6. Period of validity of licence :

Every licence under this Order, shall, unless previously suspended or cancelled, remain valid for three years from the date of its issue.

7. Renewal of licence :

(1) Every holder of licence desiring to renew the licence, shall, before the date of expiry of the licence, make an application for renewal in duplicate, to the licensing authority in Form 'C' together with a fee of rupees twenty for renewal. On receipt of such application, together with such fee, the licensing authority may renew the licence.

(2) If any application for renewal is not made before the expiry of the licence, but is made within one month from the date of expiry of the licence, the licence may be renewed on payment of additional fee of rupees twenty five, in addition to the fee for renewal of licence.

8. Dealers to display stock and price list :

Every dealer of seeds shall display in his place of business:

(a) the opening and closing stocks, on daily basis, of different seeds held by him;

(b) a list indicating prices or rates of different seeds.

9. Dealers to give memorandum to purchaser :

Every dealer shall give a cash or credit memorandum to a purchaser of seeds.

10. Power to distribute seeds :

Where it is considered necessary to do so in public interest, the Controller may, by an order in writing direct any producer or dealer to sell or distribute any seed in such manner as may be specified therein.

Enforcement Authority

11. Appointment of licensing authority :

The State Government may by notification in the Official Gazette appoint such number of persons as it thinks necessary to be licensing authority and may also define in that notification the area within which each such licensing authority shall exercise his jurisdiction.

12. Appointment of Inspectors :

The State Government may by notification in the Official Gazette appoint such number of persons as it thinks necessary to be inspectors and may in such notification define the local area within which each such Inspector shall exercise his jurisdiction.

13. Inspection and punishment :

(1) An Inspector may with a view to securing compliance with this Order-

(a) require any dealer to give any information in his possession with respect to purchase, storage and sale of seeds by him;

(b) enter upon and search any premises where any seed is stored or exhibited for sale to ensure compliance with the provisions of this Order;

(c) draw samples of seeds meant for sale, export and seeds imported, and send the same in accordance with the procedure laid down in Schedule I, to a laboratory notified under the

Seeds Act, 1966 (54 of 1966) to ensure that the sample conforms to standard of quality claimed;

(d) seize or detain any seed in respect of which he has reason to believe that a contravention of this Order has been committed or is being committed;

(e) seize any books of accounts or document relating to any seed in respect of which he has reason to believe that a contravention of this Order has been committed or is being committed.

Provided that the Inspector shall give a receipt, in respect of the books of accounts or documents seized, to the person from whom they have been seized.

Provided further that the seized books of accounts or documents shall be returned to the person from whom the same had been seized after copies thereof or extracts therefrom as certified by such person have been taken.

(2) Subject to the provision of paragraph (d) of sub-clause (1), the provision, of section 100 of the Code of Criminal Procedure, 1973 (2 of 1974) relating to search and seizure shall, so far as may be, apply to searches and seizures under this clause.

(3) Where any seed is seized by an Inspector under this clause, he shall forthwith report the fact of such seizure to a Magistrate where-upon the provisions of sections 457 and 458 of the Code of Criminal Procedure, 1973 (2 of 1974) shall, so far as may be, apply to the custody and disposal of such seed.

(4) Every person, if so required by an Inspector, shall be bound to offer all necessary facilities to him for the purpose of enabling him to exercise his power under this clause.

14. Time limit for analysis :

The laboratory to which a sample has been sent by an Inspector for analysis under this Order shall analyse the said samples and send the analysis report to the concerned Inspector within 60 days from the date of receipt of the sample in the laboratory.

15. Suspension/Cancellation of licence :

The licensing authority may, after giving the holder of the licence an opportunity of being heard, suspend or cancel the licence on the following grounds, namely:-

(a) that the licence had been obtained by misrepresentation as to a material particular; or

(b) that any of the provisions of this Order or any condition of licence has been contravened.

16. Appeal :

Any person aggrieved by an order-

(a) refusing to grant, amend or renew the licence for sale, export or import of seeds;

(b) suspending or cancelling any licence, may within sixty days from the date of the order, appeal of such authority as the State Government may specify in this behalf, and the decision of such authority shall be final. Provided that an application for appeal shall accompany an appeal fee of rupees fifty.

Miscellaneous

17. Amendment of licence :

    The licensing authority may, on receipt of a request in writing together with a fee of rupees ten from a dealer, amend the licence of such dealer.

18. Maintenance of records and submission of returns, etc. :

    (1) Every dealer shall maintain such books, accounts and records relating to his business as may be directed by the State Government.

    (2) Every dealer shall submit monthly return relating to his business for the preceding month in Form 'C' to the licensing authority by the 5th day of every month.

Sd/-

R.K. Srivastava

Joint Secretary to the Govt. of India

FORM 'A'

(See clause 4)

Form of Application to Obtain Dealer's Licence

To

The Registering Authority,

__________________ (Place)

State of/ U.T. of

1. Full name and address of the applicant:

    (a) Name and postal address:

    (b) Place of business (please give exact address):

(i) for sale

(ii) for storage

2. Is it a proprietory/partnership/Limited Company/ Hindu undivided family concern? Give the Name(s) and address(es) of proprietor/partner/ Manager/Karta.

3. In what capacity this application is made:

   (i) Proprietor

   (ii) Partner

   (iii) Manager

   (iv) Karta

4. Was the applicant ever convicted under the Essential Commodities Act, 1955 (10 of 1955), or any order issued thereunder during the last three years preceding the date of application? If so, give details.

5. Give the details of seeds to be handled.

   S.No.Name of Seed

6. I/we have deposited the licence fee of rupees fifty vide challan No. ______________ dated ______________________________ in treasury/bank ____________________

7. Declaration:

   (a) I/we declare that the information given above is true to the best of my/our knowledge and belief and no part thereof is false.

   (b) I/we have carefully read the terms and conditions of the licence given in Form 'B' appended to the Seeds (Control) Order, 1983, and agree to abide by them.

Signature of Applicant

Date: ____________

Place: ____________

Note: (1) Where the business of selling/exporting/importing seeds is intended to be carried on at more than one place, a separate licence should be obtained for each such place.

For use in the office of Licensing Authority

Date of receipt ______________

Name and designation of officer receiving the application

FORM 'B'

(See clause 5)

Licence to Carry on the Business of a dealer in Seeds

Licence No. _________ Date: ______________

Subject to the provisions of the Seeds (Control) Order, 1983 and to the terms and conditions of this Licence Shri/M/s ______________________________
is hereby granted licence to sell, export, import and store for the said purposes of seeds.

2. The licencee shall carry on the aforesaid business at ______________________ (Place for storage and place for sale) ____________________ (Tehsil or District) __________________

Date: ______________

Seal: Licensing Authority

State of ___________

Terms and conditions of licence

(i) The licence shall be displayed at a prominent and conspicuous place in a part of the business premises open to the public.

(ii) The holder of the licence shall comply with the provisions of the Seeds (Control) Order, 1983 and the notifications issued thereunder and for the time being in force.

(iii) This licence comes into force with immediate effect and shall be valid upto ____________ unless previously cancelled or suspended.

(iv) The holder of the licence shall from time to time report to the licensing authority any change in the premises where he carries on his business of sale, export, import or storage for the said purposes of seeds.

(v) The licencee shall give every facility to the licensing authority or any other officer acting under his Authority for the purpose of inspecting his stock in any shop, depot or godown or other place/places used by him for the purpose of storage, sale or export of seeds.

FORM 'C'

(See clause 7)

Application for renewal of licence to carry on the business of a dealer in seeds

To

The Licensing Authority

________________ (Place)

State of/U.T. of

I/We hereby apply for renewal of the Licence to carry on the business of dealer in seeds under the name and style of Shri/M/s. ____________________________The licence, desired to be renewed, was granted by the Licensing Authority for the State of ____________________and alloted Licence No. __________on the _____ day of __________________19

Signature of applicant(s)

Full name and address of the applicant(s) __________

Date and Place: ____________________________

Certified that the Licence bearing No. _______________ granted on __________ to carry on the business of a dealer in seeds at the premises situated _____________ is hereby renewed upto ___________, unless previously cancelled or suspended under the provisions of the Seeds (Control) Order, 1983.

Date: _____ Licensing Authority

Renewal No. _________ State of _____________

Seal:

FORM 'D'

(See clause 18)

1. Month and year:
2. Name and designation of Licensee:

(Quantity in Quintals)

Crop/ Variety	Class of seed	Opening stock on the first day of the month	Quantity purchased during the month	Total quantity imported	Total	Total quantity sold	Total quantity exported	Closing stock on the last day of the month
1	2	3	4	5	6	7	8	9
					(3+4+5)			6-(7+8)

Signature of dealer
Name: ______________
Address: ____________
____

SCHEDULE I

(See clause 13)

Sealing, Fastening, Despatch and Analysis of Samples

I. Manner of taking Samples

Samples of any seed for the purpose of analysis shall be taken in a clean dry container which shall be closed sufficiently tight to prevent leakage and entrance of moisture and shall be carefully sealed.

II. Sampling Intensity

Bulk Sampling—When sampling seed lots are stored in bulk (heaps, bins, wagons, etc.), the following sampling intensity should be regarded as a minimum requirement for obtaining the "bulk sample".

(a) upto 500 kilograms - at least 5 individual samples except in case of small lots upto 50 kilograms where a smaller number of samples is sufficient, not less than, 3 samples need be taken.

(b) 501 to 3,000 kilograms - one individual sample for each 300 kilograms, but not less than 5 individual samples.

(c) 3,001 to 20,000 kilograms - one individual sample for each 500 kilograms but not less than 10 individual samples.

For seed in bulk the individual samples should be distributed at random all over the bulk and the samples drawn from varying depths.

Bag sampling - For seed lots in bags or other containers the following sampling intensity should be regarded as a minimum requirement:

(d) upto 5 containers - sample each container but always take at least 5 individual samples.

(e) from 6 to 30 containers - sample at least one in every three containers but never less than 5.

(f) 31 containers or more - sample at least one in every five containers but never less than 10.

Unless doubt exists about the homogeneity of a lot, all such primary samples should be combined to make a composite sample of the lot for submitting to the seed testing laboratory. If the individual or primary samples are not sufficiently homogenous, they may be sent to the laboratory for a heterogeneity test.

III. Containers to be labelled and addressed —All containers containing samples for analysis shall be properly labelled and the parcels shall be properly addressed. The label on any sample of seed sent for analysis shall bear-

(a) serial number;

(b) name of the sender with official designation, if any;

(c) name of the person from whom the sample has been taken;

(d) date and place of taking the sample;

(e) kind or variety of the seed for analysis;

(f) nature and quantity of preservative, if any, added to the sample.

IV. Manner of Packing, Fastening and Scaling the Samples—All samples of seeds sent for analysis shall be packed, fastened and sealed in the following manner:

(a) The stopper shall first be securely fastened so as to prevent leakage of the containers in transit.

(b) The container shall then be completely wrapped in fairly strong thick paper. The ends of the paper shall be neatly folded in and affixed by means of gum or other adhesive.

(c) The paper cover shall be further secured by means of strong twine or thread both above and across the container, and the twine or thread shall then be fastened on the paper cover by means of sealing wax on which there shall be at least four distinct and clear impressions of the seal of the sender, of which, one shall be at the top of the packet, one at the bottom and the other two on the body of the packet. The knots of the twine or thread shall be covered by means of sealing wax bearing the impression of the seal of the sender.

4

General Aspects of Seed Policy

Policy is essentially a 'declaration of intent' by the government on how it wishes the seed sector to develop. When the government was the major or sole player in the seed sector, policy was not important, or was an automatic consequence of a larger economic and social system. However, when the system becomes more diverse and new participants enter the seed business, policy assumes a key role. It therefore has a special relevance to countries undergoing economic transition.

In fact, policy could be the key catalyst in the liberalisation process. This was demonstrated very clearly in Turkey, which announced a major policy change in the mid-1980s by encouraging foreign investment in the seed sector. India took a similar decisive step in 1990, with dramatic consequences in the ensuing decade. These examples illustrate clearly the immense impact that policies can have on the development of the seed sector.

However, policies cannot change the fundamental technical and economic characteristics of seed supply. No matter how strong the pressure for privatisation, some crops are intrinsically unprofitable and may not be taken up by the private sector. Therefore, government agencies may have a continuing strategic role in the seed system to ensure that seed of certain crops continues to be made available and that there is a channel for introducing new varieties. Here again, Turkey provides a good example of this dilemma.

Despite the strong encouragement of private sector participation, certain crops, notably wheat, remain largely in the public sector, with state farms and cooperatives still playing a major role in these crops. Moreover, in countries with unpredictable climate, there may also be a seed security element to consider, so that government institutions can be the 'default supplier' in times of crop failure. It is impossible for the private sector to accept that responsibility because of the financial risks involved.

Changing Role of Government in Seed Supply

In socialist economies, the government was the only effective supplier of seed, through its central planning of the economy. The current perception is that the role of government is to create a favourable 'policy environment' within which other suppliers can develop the commercial market. This concept therefore provides the justification for developing a seed policy that can achieve those objectives. We may consider the analogy of the garden - in the past, large public organisations occupied all the space and this left no room for anything else to grow. Nowadays, the objective is to create a fertile garden in which different types of enterprises may develop according to their competitive advantage.

Policy and legislation

It is important to distinguish between policy and legislation. Nearly all countries have seed laws and technical regulations controlling certain aspects of the variety and seed system. This is intended to protect the various participants, both producers and farmers, and typically covers:

- — testing and registration of varieties;
- — seed quality standards - typically through 'certification' procedures;
- — registration of companies and facilities involved in processing and marketing seed;
- — labelling requirements on seed packages - linked to certification; and
- — protecting the property rights of plant breeders.

Such legislation can exist quite independently of any seed policy; it applies to all seed and varieties marketed within the country, whether originating from government agencies or private companies. Policies, in contrast, are not part of the law: they are intended rather to establish certain basic guidelines for the operation of the sector. For example, the policy may say that regulations should apply in the same way to varieties from public and private sources. Therefore policy is separate from laws and regulations but should be in harmony with them. In the case of seed, the policy may be more concerned with ensuring that regulations are applied in an equitable way and without hidden discrimination. We may consider that there is hierarchy of official interventions, namely policy, laws, regulations and procedures, as represented in Figure 1.

Policy Management

Besides setting up the policy initially, it is essential to monitor its impact and to make adjustments as necessary. Stability is a key feature of policies if they are to generate confidence among the various players in the market, but there should still be a forum for discussing policy issues and suggesting changes. This should be a responsibility of an 'apex body' of some kind, such as a National Seed Council or Board, which meets perhaps 2 or 3 times a year to review all aspects of the seed industry. This must be a truly representative body, including the private sector, in contrast to the past, where such committees were dominated by government officials and research organisations. The existence and role of this apex body should be defined in the policy, and also in the Seed Law. There is also a need to ensure that policy is implemented in practice. Sometimes the policy says the right things, but those who implement regulations and procedures lower down the pyramid continue to apply old and discriminatory measures, sometimes for reasons of self-interest because proposed reforms may threaten their employment.

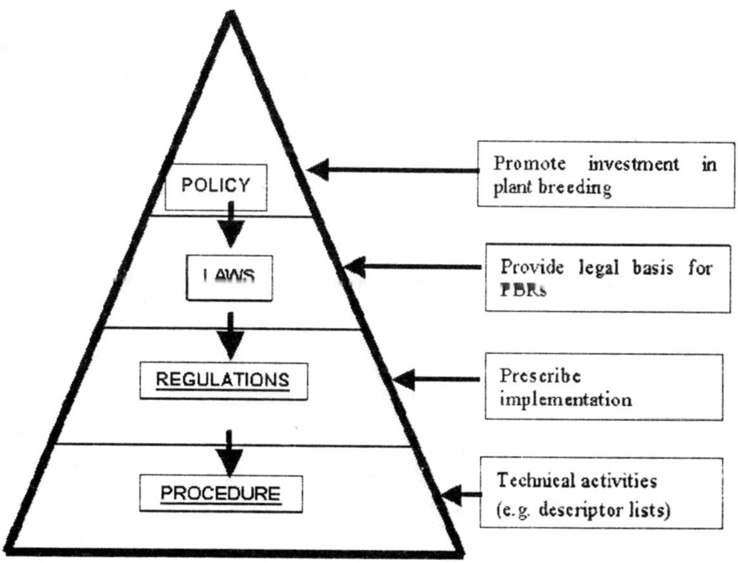

Figure 1. The intervention hierarchy - with an example from plant variety protection

Ensuring representation

If policy changes are successful in promoting a more commercial seed supply system, how does the emerging private sector ensure that its views and needs are adequately represented to Government? Individual companies may have their own channels of communication, but ideally there should be a truly representative mechanism for discussing matters of mutual interest within the private sector. This function is normally achieved by a 'National Seed Association' supported by the member companies and with access to policy-makers at a high level. This has been an important element of the seed industry in developed countries, where 'trade associations' of all kinds have a long history. This structure is also reflected in the membership of the International Seed Trade Federation (FIS), which is primarily composed of National Seed Associations, not of individual companies.

In recent years, we have seen the establishment of such national seed associations in several countries in the region served by ICARDA, notably in Turkey, Morocco, Egypt and Pakistan. This is a very positive development, as it can provide the seed industry with a formal voice and a channel for communication to Government. It may therefore be an element of the seed policy to promote and recognise such a body. At the regional level also, new seed associations have been established, notably for the Asia and Pacific Region (APSA) in 1994 and for Africa (AFSTA) in 2000.

Functions of Seed Policy

One vital function of a seed policy is to define 'who does what' within the more open and diverse system that is evolving. As already noted, this was not an issue when the government did almost everything itself, but, with the liberalisation of many economies, seed policies have become much more important. The new policy may therefore be a catalyst for initial change and a guardian of the transition process. It should ensure that the playing field remains reasonably level, and certainly not discriminate against 'new entrants' to the seed sector during their establishment phase.

Access to Facilities and Services

This applies particularly to quality control procedures, which, in the short term, will remain mostly in Government hands. If new enterprises of any kind enter the market, they may not initially have their own quality control facilities. It may be more efficient for them to use the existing facilities operated by government agencies. This is a logical approach, but it requires absolutely that their needs are being met on an equal basis. If, for example, the seed samples from a local seed cooperative are always left until other, traditional, clients have been satisfied, then the system is being discriminatory. If new entrants to the system are to be encouraged, then they must clearly be treated in an equitable way. Another possibility for such open access is the leasing of existing processing facilities to new enterprises.

Access to Public Varieties

This is an important topic, but one which varies according to the actual situation in different countries. If the research system is still in the public sector, then it is necessary to devise a mechanism by which those varieties can be made more widely available, rather than just passing automatically to a public seed organisation. There are various ways in which this can be done, such as by offering licences to multiply new varieties. The continuation of public sector breeding is potentially a stimulus to the emergence of a new seed industry, since companies are unlikely to set up breeding programmes initially, and may need to obtain new varieties from elsewhere to strengthen their portfolio. However, an equitable policy for accessing these varieties must be devised and, in the context of plant variety protection, a royalty payment may also be expected.

Variety Release and Introduction

One of the features of centrally-planned agriculture was its reliance on a few varieties, which were sown on very large areas. This was perhaps a matter of convenience in specifying cultivation procedures, but it also often reflected the relatively small number of varieties that satisfied the criterion of wide adaptation. The same situation can be found in government-dominated seed programmes in many developing countries, where, despite large-scale breeding and evaluation, relatively few varieties were actually listed and the procedures for such listing were often very lengthy. Indeed, this situation still persists in many countries, and it is regrettable for several reasons, in particular as it reduces the return on research investment by delaying the uptake of new varieties, and it deprives farmers of the choice that would enable them to exercise flexibility in their management practices. Of course, such flexibility was not encouraged in centrally-planned agriculture.

A related issue is the introduction and release of varieties from other countries. The lengthy testing and stringent release conditions mentioned above may also apply to foreign varieties, but that is especially wasteful if they those varieties are already being grown successfully in similar environments. At its worst, this practice may simply be a way of favouring the national breeding programme by making it harder for introduced varieties to reach the market. This again reduces farmers' choice and potentially deprives them of varieties that could meet their needs very effectively. For this reason, cooperation in variety testing would be a very positive regional dimension in seed policy.

Prices and Subsidies

The previous socialist system was highly subsidised, so there was no direct relationship between costs and prices: everything was simply administered according to the Plan. With the move towards a market economy, there is a natural expectation of charging to a market price, which covers at least the direct costs of production. This is certainly a desirable objective, but of course it may also be difficult to achieve because the production units were often inefficient and they did not have to consider cost control. The sudden imposition of market obligations on previously subsidised state institutions may be unrealistic, and, if enforced, may simply lead to rapid bankruptcy, which has happened in some countries. At the same time, if subsidies continue, then it will be very difficult for new entrants from the private sector to compete on price, and, furthermore, they may be discouraged from even starting because they are uncertain about government intentions.

Therefore, the question of pricing is one of the most sensitive issues in the re-structuring process. The policy should lay down guidelines that promote equal treatment for all, but the implementation of this should also be monitored. Complete collapse of the former system, without any new growth to replace it, may have a disastrous effect, and indeed that is the situation observed in some countries. Although the private sector has moved in to colonise some sectors of the economy, in general that has not been the case in agriculture because of the risks and low returns on investment. There are more attractive areas of the economy for private capital.

Related Issues

Future of Research Institutions

The place of research institutions within the re-structured agriculture and seed sector deserves special attention. A convenient solution is to say that these institutions now have to become market-oriented and to survive on income generated by the products of their research. While this may be a very desirable goal, it may also be unrealistic in practice, because they do not have a product portfolio sufficient to support the research infrastructure, even with some drastic pruning. The 'Seed Associations' of the former Yugoslavia were a classic model of how to link breeding research to the market and achieve full cost recovery. However, that approach worked well in only a few crops, especially maize and sunflower, that are highly profitable. It is unlikely that small research institutes will suddenly become self-financing. The writer believes that this has been tried in Poland over the past ten years, but there have been many casualties.

In these circumstances, the government may be forced to decide whether it wishes to allow these research centres to perish, or whether to support them from the central budget, if they have some strategic importance. It may certainly be risky to abandon the research system to a market fate. In the long term, plant variety protection and royalties may provide the solution to this issue, but in the interim, expecting significant revenue may be optimistic in view of the poor economic status of agriculture in so many countries. Furthermore, there may be legitimate concerns in abandoning national breeding capability and thus becoming totally dependent on foreign suppliers for both varieties and seed.

Future of quality control services

The possibility of cost-recovery is raised frequently in the context of quality control (QC) agencies. In some European countries, there has been a steady trend in this direction so that nowadays some such agencies are virtually self-financing from charges levied for their services. There are two problems with this approach in the countries represented here. First, the existing QC services are often large, because of the comprehensive service they provided in the past: this makes them relatively costly and inefficient. Second, seed producers may be reluctant to pay the charges because this is another element that has to be covered in the selling price. To summarise, cost recovery is a good principle, because it makes both service providers and clients more alert to the efficiency and value of the service they get. In practice, however, it may have to be implemented cautiously to stand any chance of success.

Development of extension services

The absence of organised extension services was one of the most notable features of the agricultural sector in centrally-planned economies. This function was assumed partly by general recommendations for crop husbandry, and locally by specialist technicians within the production units. The lack of a diverse community of farmers, and the lack of managerial flexibility at the farm level, largely removed the need for this service. With the diversification of agriculture during economic transition, there is a need to provide information, and this prompts the establishment of an extension facility of some kind.

The immediate problem is that this is an additional responsibility that governments will find difficult to finance from their limited budgets. This is a serious constraint, because the emerging community of 'new farmers' may need both management and technical advice to establish their businesses. Whatever arrangements are made in different countries to address this need, information about varieties and seed quality will be a key component. Familiar activities, such as on-farm trials, demonstrations and field days, will all have a part to play in this process. When the private sector does start to take over a significant proportion of the seed supply, it would be an intrinsic part of their marketing operations to provide information and to organise promotional activities.

International Dimensions in Seed Policy

Policy is essentially a national concern, promoted by individual governments for their own territories. However, there are also external considerations, both regionally in relation to the adjacent countries, and globally, relating to the international seed industry and those organisations involved in it. Some parts of the seed trade are now so internationalised that very few countries can pursue a policy of independence and self-sufficiency. Certainly, within the region under discussion at this meeting, only one or two of the larger countries could adopt that approach, while the majority will depend on substantial trans-border movements of seed.

Climate for Foreign Participation and Investment

There are several different mechanisms by which foreign expertise and material can be used to develop the seed sector. These range from simple importation of pre-packed seeds (typically of vegetables), through to major investment or joint ventures undertaking the full range of activities, including breeding, production and marketing. The climate for receiving inbound investment may vary greatly depending on general financial regulations as well as market opportunities. We would consider that inward investment is a positive factor because it demonstrates commitment and confidence in the market. However, countries might wish to impose some conditions about local participation in such ventures to ensure mutual benefit and promote continuity in such commercial relationships.

Participation in International Organisations

During the time of the Soviet Union, COMECON provided a massive integrated group of economies working on broadly the same system. There were formalised internal supply channels, though not on a truly commercial basis. For example, Kyrgyzstan and southern Kazakhstan produced seed of forages, especially alfalfa, for export to other countries in Eastern Europe and the Baltic States. There was a significant volume of movement, but all administered internally and with no element of competitive marketing.

This network collapsed with the break up of the Soviet Union, and it would be very difficult to restore, because there are many other suppliers in the international market who can quickly take that business, and have done so. However, ultimately, some countries of the region do have a comparative advantage in seed production, as indeed Hungary has had for many years, exporting to many western countries. Therefore, despite the recent interruptions in trade, countries in this region will eventually find their place within the international seed trade, both as producers and importers, depending upon their needs and comparative advantage.

With that prospect, it is essential that they begin (or resume) participation in the various international organisations that facilitate that trade, namely FIS, ISTA, OECD and UPOV. Unfortunately, that may present funding difficulties because of the costs of participation. Here again, a regional association might assist individual countries by developing links of that kind and providing information to members in the way that the 'WANA Seed Network' does from ICARDA for some 20 countries in West Asia and North Africa.

Procedures and Standards

Harmonisation is probably one of the most important technical aspects of seed policy, although it is difficult to implement unless there is some forum for coordination. The members of the European Union have had common (although not identical) procedures for many years in respect of seed. The most important aspects relate to the quality standards required for marketing seed and for variety testing and listing procedures, since there is a Common Catalogue of varieties. As a result, both varieties and seed can move within the EU with relative ease, using a uniform labelling format recognised in all countries. The actual standards adopted have to be agreed among all the participants, and that may cause difficulties initially, as happened in the EU. However, in this region, because many countries had a common background, such harmonisation should not be too difficult. It is perhaps more important that countries do not start taking divergent paths, thus making harmonisation and re-integration more complicated.

As already noted, regional groups of countries should certainly consider the coordinated testing of varieties, particularly in Central Asia, where complex national boundaries overlay uniform agro-ecological areas. It would be very efficient for these countries to coordinate their variety assessment trials so that data from many locations could be combined within a single analysis. Regional variety lists, whether for regulatory or advisory purposes, would therefore be a very positive development.

Plant variety protection is another activity that would benefit from regional coordination, such as by agreeing to share data and extend rights between participating countries. This inspired the establishment of the European Community Variety Rights Office, thus enabling breeders to obtain variety rights for all countries of the Union on the basis of a single application and test.

Regional Seed Policy Initiatives

If the countries of this region are preparing or implementing policies to guide the development of their seed industries during the period of economic transition, then some mechanism for regional coordination would be very desirable. In the case of the westward-looking countries, any policies they devise should be based on convergence with the standards of the European Union, both for commercial benefit and to ease the path towards eventual membership, if desired.

For the Central Asian and Caucasus countries, the European Union may not be the determining factor, but still some regional coordination would be highly desirable for reasons already outlined. Given the various regional dimensions noted above, the Central Asian countries might benefit particularly from a regional initiative of this kind, because of their complex national frontiers, which bear no relation to agriculture.

Role of Private Companies in the Seed Production and Distribution Systems

The writer is grateful for the opportunity to address this meeting on the subject of the last ten years of the Hungarian seed sector, during the period since the change of regime, with special regard to the problems encountered during privatisation. In addition to aspects specific to Hungary, much experience was gained that could be of use in other countries where privatisation is now in progress or is still in the initial phases. The writer should like to provide food for thought, since the aim of this meeting is to discuss how the regional development of the seed sector could be accelerated.

The privatisation of the seed sector in Hungary was decisively influenced by:

- — seed production and trading traditions,
- — the privatisation of agriculture, and particularly of the food industry,
- — the privatisation of the whole of the national economy, and
- — trends in agricultural exports.

One important characteristic of Hungarian seed privatisation was that it was based, to a large extent, on the existing traditions of seed production and trading. In many respects, it is simply a continuation of these traditions under altered conditions. This will become clear if we cast a look at the history of Hungarian agriculture. As early as the second half of the nineteenth century, it was recognised that the ecological potential of Hungary, the varied soil conditions, the continental climate, the cheap labour and the logistic advantages all favoured seed production and seed trading. Investors were well aware of this potential, which was supported by the government to such an extent that high quality could be achieved despite the political conflicts.

Variety testing, registration and seed analysis began under state supervision throughout the country, agricultural research institutes were set up, experts were sent to study abroad, new plant species and varieties were tested on large estates within the framework of a seed campaign, and in 1895 a seed law was passed that was equivalent to legislation elsewhere in Europe and which remained in force until 1968. In such an environment, the seed trade flourished and sales were brisk both at home and abroad.

Hungarian seed, especially seed of lucerne, designated by a white label with the Hungarian national colours of red, white and green, became a household word. By the end of the nineteenth century, seed production and trading was already much as we know it today and was an important branch of the economy. This development continued into the first half of the twentieth century. It is enough to note that Hungary was a founder member of FIS and ISTA, in which organisations it played an active role. Hungary was one of the leading partners in the international seed trade. There were, of course, problems, and agricultural crises. It is very instructive to study the measures taken to solve the crisis of 1929-33.

In 1931, the government elaborated a wheat production programme aimed at maintaining or, if possible, enhancing the traditionally high quality of Hungarian wheat, while at the same time achieving the greatest possible yield. This ideal was personified by the variety Bánkúti 1201, the general cultivation of which was supported by the government through a free, later reduced-price, seed campaign. At the same time, wheat production of the country was mapped to determine which varieties were most suited to production in the various growing districts, and care was also taken to ensure that sufficient wheat was milled to satisfy domestic requirements. The concepts which marked this period are still valid, namely the encouragement of high seed quality, state subsidies for seed, and the consideration of individual growing districts and the whole of the production chain.

The practice of contracted seed production was introduced in the first half of the twentieth century. This meant that seed merchants from Western Europe, chiefly from the UK, the Netherlands, Germany and Denmark, brought basic seed of their own peas, beans and flowers to Hungary for seed production, since they were assured that the quality of the new seed would be excellent and they could thus hope for a larger share of the market and higher profits. The volume and wide variety of the seed exported by Hungary can be seen in Table 1.

Even more important than the volume of exports, however, was the development of a broad spectrum of stable business contacts, the real value of which was felt during the difficult years following the Second World War. By this time the seed sector had become a well-established branch of the economy, and its reputation was enhanced by the excellent results achieved by Hungarian plant breeders and by the extremely sound institutional background (seed testing and certification). The well-managed large estates excelled in the production of field crops, while the small- and medium-sized farms achieved success in the production of vegetable and flower seeds. Seed had become a traditional product of Hungarian agriculture.

Table 1. Hungarian seed exports 1925 - 1939 (tonnes)

Year	Beans, peas, lentils	Vetch	Lupins	Millet, mustard, sorghum	Oil-seeds	Lucerne	Red and white clover	Sugar beet seed	Vegetable and flower seed	Grass seed	Total
1925	34 967	1 319	328	9 218	25 638	326	2 732	62	277	43	74 910
1926	67 095	695	222	4 592	23 334	483	2 625	61	240	29	99 376
1927	33 619	1 884	255	2 962	23 463	1 366	3 397	37	277	28	67 288
1928	16 327	1 729	314	2 100	15 526	1 218	2 718	179	405	22	41 038
1929	31 257	1 098	404	4 958	25 674	994	3 347	363	701	66	68 862
1930	17 661	1 700	2 818	2 947	27 886	1 260	3 940	302	786	108	59 408
1931	15 446	1 352	679	917	19 187	2 031	4 145	445	791	82	45 075
1932	18 775	3 705	226	1 368	15 796	2 991	5 787	163	711	68	49 590
1933	35 751	1 932	511	1 728	22 580	2 409	5 757	142	1 323	132	72 265
1934	34 280	2 932	1 569	3 190	16 382	2 329	4 874	932	895	85	67 468
1935	28 008	2 220	772	4 152	20 898	2 009	6 490	352	1 220	44	66 174
1936	29 841	5 810	2 152	3 380	15 601	3 426	10 869	110	990	55	72 234
1937	52 603	11 218	2 244	16 092	15 719	3 417	12 026	288	1 347	61	115 015
1938	32 016	6 361	1 167	4 690	15 600	1 007	11 017	407	1 096	143	73 504
1939	31 470	6 046	2 290	1 563	12 799	2 275	8 172	1 570	1 135	312	67 632

The losses suffered during the Second World War, the payment of reparations, changes in ownership relationships and nationalisation - all these conspired to ruin the seed sector. Socialist trade organisations were set up, including the Seed Production and Marketing Company and the Trading Office for State Farms (ÁGKER), which were responsible for the supervision and execution of state-controlled seed production and trading. Seed exports were arranged by the foreign trade company AGRIMPEX. It is interesting to note that while agricultural contacts with capitalist countries ceased in the tense political atmosphere of the Cold War years, the seed trade was, to a certain extent, an exception. In 1950, for instance, 1 619 t of lucerne seed and 200 t of spring vetch seed were exported, thanks to the goodwill built up by correct business contacts during the previous period. In 1953-54, contracts were signed again by British, German, French and Dutch firms for the production of seed.

The Hungarian seed trade gradually regained its old positions on foreign seed markets and managed to reach the 1938 export level by 1970. It is important to note that although Hungary's membership in international organisations was suspended, contacts with FIS and ISTA were maintained, and due to the foreign trade relations, Hungarian experts were kept well informed of the situation in seed production in Europe and throughout the world. At the same time, forward-looking Hungarian agricultural policy-makers were able to get a hybrid maize programme started in 1958.

A whole series of seed plants were built as part of a priority state investment for the processing of hybrid maize seed. In 1960, hybrid maize seed was produced for the German firm Nord Saat, but the real boom started in 1968, with the announcement of the programme known as the new economic mechanism, which ushered in the golden decade of Hungarian agriculture, during which agricultural production was doubled. This was also true of the seed sector. In 1968, a new seed law was passed introducing an open variety policy, which meant that variety owners from all over the world could market seed of their varieties in Hungary after state testing and registration, though at the time this was still only possible through state agencies.

In 1970, when Hungary acceded to the OECD seed registration system, which was obligatory for many seed exports to the West, Hungarian seed was present on the market in 25 capitalist countries, involving over one hundred regular purchasers and importers. Hungary also became a member of the Seed Specialisation Agreement, operated by the Council for Mutual Economic Aid (COMECON), and supplied substantial quantities of seed, mostly of hybrid maize, to the Soviet Union and other socialist countries. In 1975, the dynamically expanding seed sector gained even greater momentum due to the appearance of major American and Canadian seed companies, such as Pioneer, Dekalb, Cargill and Asgrow, and to increased activity by West European firms.

The introduction of modern, high-yielding hybrid maize varieties; new production technologies; up-to-date machinery, especially tractors, combines, seed drills and sprayers; and modern seed dryers, resulted in enormous developments. The existing seed plants were modernised and expanded using western technology, and new, up-to-date seed plants were built. Foreign firms could only do business in Hungary through the designated state companies, such as AGRIMPEX, INTERCOOPORESEN and HUNGAROSEED, and they were generally based in breeding institutes (Szeged, Martonvásár, Iregszemcse) or sometimes in large production systems (IKR, KITE,

KSZE). The seed trade was also modernised, with foreign trade being the responsibility of the HUNGAROSEED company set up in 1981, and comprising 12 large farms, as well as the Seed Production and Trading Company and the Trading Office for State Farms (ÁGKER). The members were granted a collective foreign trading licence, allowing them to participate in the drafting of business contracts and to maintain contacts with foreign partners. The latter was extremely important, as it led to the acquisition of a considerable amount of expertise, which was then utilised in Hungary and in some cases further developed.

In 1983, Hungary signed the UPOV Agreement, thus recognising variety ownership rights and origin protection, the internationally accepted system of variety identification. In the meantime, courses had been re-started for the training of seed experts, plant geneticists and breeders, and skilled workers, technicians and laboratory staff for the seed plants. All in all, it can be said that between 1960 and 1990, professional and technical knowledge of seed production and processing was concentrated in the best-equipped state farms and cooperatives and in companies specialising in seed production and trading. Seed production was carried out on large, well-cultivated fields. The homogeneous quality that could be achieved on these large fields, and the isolation ensured in the case of open-pollinated plant species, were a great advantage.

After initial difficulties, plant breeding attained excellent results, especially in the development of cereals (particularly winter wheat), sunflower, and traditional Hungarian crops such as lucerne, clover and spice peppers, and in the elaboration of production technologies specific to the varieties. The breeding institutes were also in state ownership and were supervised by the Ministry of Agriculture and Food Industry, the Hungarian Academy of Sciences, the agricultural universities and colleges, or the Seed Production and Trading Company.

There was virtually no private ownership in the seed sector, except for a few nurseries producing fruit trees and ornamentals. However, in order to compensate the rural population for the higher costs of electricity and transport and for the poor state of public supplies, and to improve public morale, those working in state farms or as members of cooperatives were allowed to farm on plots of 0.4-0.6 ha, and these were often used to produce seed or propagation stock under the supervision of the large-scale farms.

The income gained from these plots of land was not subject to any deductions. The large farms delegated the production of hybrid maize and hybrid sunflower seed, which required a great deal of conscientious labour, to the people farming these plots. The farm workers and cooperative members were glad to take on this task (which usually meant involving the whole family in the work), as the extra income was considerable.

The multiplication of vegetable and flower seed was mostly carried out in the gardens of seed company employees (all the village houses had sufficient land for this purpose), but seed cleansing and sales could only take place through state companies. The importance of this situation became clear after the change of regime, since it meant that many agricultural workers had a good working knowledge of seed production.

In the 1980s, the seed sector was characterised by a negligible ratio of private ownership, but by the presence of all the major seed companies of the USA, Canada and Western Europe. Although the foreign firms did not have the right to produce, process or sell seed directly (their Hungarian partners naturally paid the agreed royalties punctually), they were very well acquainted with the situation of the Hungarian seed sector and with the seed markets to which Hungarian seed was exported, and also had wide-ranging personal contacts. Seed production for export purposes and the presence of foreign seed companies in Hungary had a beneficial effect on the technical and professional standard of the whole of the Hungarian seed production chain.

The high genetic, biological and technical seed quality required by the foreign firms, the importance attached to package size and appearance, the introduction of new laboratory methods for seed testing (e.g. cold test, electrophoresis), and the need for punctual, precise delivery - all these had a favourable effect on the multiplication, processing and sales of Hungarian seed and on the whole of field crop production. The importance of the seed sector can be seen in Table 2.

In the 1980s, seed production was carried out on 300 000-350 000 ha (7.0-7.3% of the arable area), which was greater than the seed multiplication area of France, the largest seed producer in the European Union, and seed exports amounted to 150 000-160 000 t, which was 25% of total seed production. Hungary was the largest seed producer in the socialist bloc. When the change of regime began, Hungary already had a modern seed sector, with wide-ranging international contacts and a good knowledge of seed markets, not only within the socialist bloc, but also in the West.

The change of regime also brought fundamental changes in agriculture. Political and social transformations were given priority and were carried out rapidly and democratically. There were plenty of examples in history for this process. There were none, however, to show how the socialist economic system could be converted into a market economy, and this transformation went much more slowly and proved much more difficult than was foreseen.

Table 2. Major annual data on seed multiplication

Year	Inspected seed multiplication area (ha)	Quantity of certified seed sold			Total (tonne)
		At home (tonne)	Abroad (tonne)	(%)	
1962	128 500	-	-	-	378 600
1972	271 400	-	-	-	396 400
1982	330 128	454 054	112 384	19.8	566 439
1983	312 774	452 464	123 854	21.4	576 318
1984	334 427	463 886	112 677	19.5	576 563
1985	344 784	465 710	144 878	23.7	610 588
1986	328 826	447 937	149 815	25.0	597 752
1987	309 300	462 744	147 907	24.2	610 651
1988	333 546	457 782	131 469	22.3	589 251
1989	307 893	420 165	149 709	26.3	569 874
1990	278 219	345 209	97 155	21.9	442 364
1991	239 634	230 593	81 110	26.0	311 703
1992	169 992	247 624	91 117	26.8	338 741
1993	158 995	291 971	88 337	23.2	380 308
1994	180 286	260 112	84 351	24.5	344 463
1995	181 975	219 465	95 164	30.2	314 629
1996	160 457	241 675	74 628	23.5	316 303
1997	155 775	294 390	79 605	21.3	373 995
1998	180 363	252 481	82 526	24.6	335 007
1999	169 092	232 751	81 762	25.9	314 513
2000	156 400				

In agriculture, the question of land, the most important factor in production, was dealt with by the Compensation Law, while the wealth acquired by the cooperatives was the subject of the Cooperative Law. The peculiarity of this law was that it did not achieve real privatisation. Many people became the owners of small plots of land, and the lack of capital that had previously been characteristic of agriculture became even worse.

The institutional structure of centralised, state-controlled purchasing and distributing companies ceased to function, since the state withdrew from the economy, foreign markets, especially those of the COMECON countries, collapsed, and even the domestic market declined due to the massive loss of jobs. Hungarian agriculture had previously produced 50% more than was required for domestic consumption. The loss of foreign markets and the dwindling of domestic demand led to huge overproduction, and the already perceptible recession deepened into an agricultural crisis. Insolvency and an inflation rate higher than the interest rate combined to worsen the shock, with increasing numbers of bankruptcies in agriculture. Hungarian agriculture was left alone with its problems. It was against this background that the new economic laws were passed.

The most important of these was the law governing business companies, which principally favoured foreign investors who were already based in the country or had close business relationships with Hungary, and who not only had sufficient capital to take long-term risks, but also had a well-thought-out marketing strategy that allowed them to take advantage of the opportunities offered by the overproduction shock. Hungarian investments were almost non-existent due to the lack of real privatisation, the lack of capital and the extremely limited loans available. It should be noted, however, that land could not be sold to foreign individuals or companies.

The privatisation of the more profitable sections of the food industry took place extremely rapidly: the manufacture of vegetable oil, sugar and confectionery, fruit and vegetable processing, the manufacture of soft drinks and tobacco products, and to a certain extent the dairy, meat and poultry industries and the manufacture of feed. To put it bluntly, the privatisation of the food industry meant that the farmers suddenly found themselves in a defenceless situation. The disparity between agricultural costs and returns was increasing rapidly, with the cost of inputs, in terms of plant protection chemicals, machinery, fertilisers, fuel and services, approaching or reaching Western standards, while - with the exception of 2000 - wholesale and retail prices rose slowly or stagnated, and in 1998-99 even dropped.

Mention must also be made of the fate of the state farms, the majority of which have been liquidated, since the land they managed was privatised under the terms of the Compensation Law, and the new owners either started farming themselves or leased the land to other farmers or farming organisations. The Company Law stipulated that companies in state ownership, such as state farms, should also be converted into shareholding companies. This was not just a formal transformation, but a real one, since it put control of the companies in the hands of a board of directors delegated by the owners (although in many cases the State Privatisation and Property Management Company had majority ownership, the companies were part-owned by the local council or by the employees), and the work of the management was supervised by a supervisory board. Some companies were purchased by the management and the employees. Interestingly enough, after a few abortive attempts, foreign capital did not show any serious interest in the state-owned farms, since the Hungarian laws did not allow them to buy the land or to acquire long-term leases. The government recognised the magnitude of the agricultural crisis and the importance of safe food supplies in general and of biological resources in particular, since these are of great significance for the future. For this reason, 26 agricultural shareholding companies were placed under long-term state ownership. These companies were chiefly farms operating seed processing plants, producing breeding animals, or reliably producing large quantities of high standard milk, meat, poultry, eggs or fish, in most cases profitably.

In general, with the exception of a few cases, such as the Compensation Law and the Cooperative Law, which were based on political and social factors rather than on sound economic considerations, privatisation was carried out according to the laws of the market economy. It is now clear, however, that the spontaneous transformation of the economy was overestimated, and the difficulties involved, especially the length of time the transformation would take, were not correctly evaluated.

In Hungry, the change of regime also caused structural alterations in the seed sector. Changes in ownership rights, the sudden flaring up of the agricultural crisis, the loss of foreign markets, the wave of bankruptcies, the insolvency and the high rate of inflation plunged the seed sector into a critical situation. The foreign trade companies, which had formally enjoyed a monopoly, and the companies responsible for domestic trading proved incapable of adjusting to the rapid changes, because management was too bureaucratic, cumbersome and slow. The foreign companies that had exploited the possibilities offered by the Company Law and were already present in Hungary adjusted quickly to the new situation. They established subsidiaries in Hungary and, since their varieties already had a good reputation, they were able to gain a strong foothold, because they not only had an excellently elaborated marketing strategy for the well-known market, but were also in possession of experience and capital. When the political and social situation stabilised, these foreign companies gained even more ground.

Table 3. Trends in seed exports and imports (US$ '000)

Year	*Export*	*Import*
1992	81 992	19 872
1993	94 033	39 320
1994	95 517	36 224
1995	86 653	36 085
1996	72 701	31 666
1997	59 528	24 130
1998	64 953	33 730
1999	66 840	28 919

The agricultural shareholding companies retained in state ownership also adapted rapidly and flexibly to the changes. They set up export companies to ensure a stable market for the hybrid maize and sunflower they produced, and also managed to compete with the foreign companies on the home market. Looking back, it can be said that the agricultural shareholding companies that remained under state ownership did their job successfully. This is backed up by statistical data. According to Table 2, the amount of certified seed exported in 1990 dropped by 65%, but it can be seen from Table 3, and especially from Table 4, that although hybrid maize seed markets were lost in East Germany, Czechoslovakia and Poland, Hungarian agriculture achieved a unique success on the CIS market: in 1992-93 and in 1994 more seed of higher value was exported to CIS countries than to members of the European Union.

It is worth taking a closer look at this success story, as there is much to be learnt from it. Within COMECON, the Seed Specialisation Agreement provided the framework for important business contacts. In addition, many young people from CIS countries, especially from Russia, studied at the University of Agricultural Sciences in Gödöllö, and even more Hungarian specialists attended university in Russia or the Ukraine. Some then married there, and in many cases had successful careers. This meant that Hungary had accurate knowledge of the size and special nature of the CIS market, and could provide very competitive, super-early maize hybrids and super-early hybrid sunflower seed with reliable genetic, biological and technical quality in packs to Western standards. Extremely successful demonstrations were held, the production technology was provided and symposiums were organised.

This flourishing business received a setback in 1996, when American rivals began to distribute seed within the framework of an aid programme, with a credit construction backed up by state guarantees, which the Hungarian partners were unable to equal, since the Hungarian state budget was not in a position to shoulder the risks. It is worth noting, however, that in spring 1997, Hungarian seed merchants did business in 10 of the 12 climatic zones in Russia, where 18 Hungarian and 2 Russian-Hungarian joint hybrids were registered, while

11 Hungarian maize hybrids were on the national list in the Ukraine and 3 in Belarus. In addition, the Seed Agreement signed in the town of Biszkek was ratified by the Hungarian government.

Role of National and Foreign Seed Companies

Hungary continued to produce seed on behalf of German, French and Dutch companies. Most of the lost East German, Czech, Slovakian and Polish markets were supplied with hybrid maize seed produced in Hungary, but the distributor was, of course, the variety owner.

The agricultural shareholding companies that remained under long-term state ownership also play a substantial role in Hungarian seed production and distribution, since the production and sales of seed from self-pollinating crops, especially cereals, fodder crops and legumes, has largely remained the sphere of Hungarian companies, and the breeding of winter wheat is exhibiting dynamic development. It must be emphasized again, however, that these modernised companies with majority state ownership had to fight hard for their markets and were obliged to adjust rapidly and flexibly to the new situations arising during the changes.

As mentioned earlier, the monopoly previously enjoyed by the state companies trading seed on foreign and domestic markets had been terminated. In the course of the transformation, a number of smaller companies were set up, generally with the participation of foreign capital, while some parts of the sector were bought up entirely by foreign companies. These new companies rationalised their activities to comply with the changed situation. They organised domestic seed production and distribution, they produced seed for foreign firms, and acted as dealers for the large foreign companies, and in some cases also for Hungarian firms. In many cases, they

Table 4. Seed exports from Hungary to various regions, 1993-99

Region	1993		1994		1995		1996		1997		1998		1999
	%	*value*	%	*value*	%	*value*	%	*value*	%	*value*	%	*value*	*value*
CIS	47.58	44 744	42.01	40 132	38.30	33 194	8.11	5 900	18.61	11 080	5.88	3 823	5 389
CEFTA	2.91	2 743	5.06	4 834	4.53	3 930	5.64	4 102	9.21	5 484	14.31	9 301	10 783
EU	42.29	39 775	42.29	40 402	50.54	43 796	79.61	57 882	64.10	38 160	62.57	40 642	41 541
Other	7.20	6 771	10.62	10 149	6.61	5 733	6.62	4 817	8.07	4 804	17.22	11 187	9 127
Total	100.00	94 033	100.00	95 517	100.00	86 653	100.00	72 701	100.00	59 528	100.00	64 953	66 840

expanded their activities to include the production and export of industrial crops, alternative crops or plants suitable for use as birdseed.

Many of the highly educated specialists from the old state companies, who had a knowledge of languages and good business contacts both at home and abroad, set up private companies and became seed merchants, either as dealers or as the Hungarian representatives of foreign companies, for whom they organised seed production. There are between 50 and 80 such private companies. In general, development is limited in these companies due to the slow accumulation of capital. With the stabilisation of the political, social and economic situation, the participation of foreign capital is gradually strengthening, with new developments being made. In mixed-ownership companies, this often means that the shareholding of the Hungarian owners is reduced, since they are unable to keep pace with this process.

Special attention should be drawn to the enormous developments carried out by the large multinational companies - Pioneer, Novartis and Seminis - over the last five years. In 1996, Pioneer built the most up-to-date seed plant in eastern central Europe, in the Hungarian town of Szarvas. This plant has an annual seed processing capacity of 24,000 t. Seminis and Novartis have established up-to-date logistic centres and laboratories, and have modernised Hungarian seed plants. Many foreign companies now have nurseries in Hungary to test the varieties of the future.

Final User-driven Process

A separate chapter should also be devoted to analysing the effect exerted on the seed sector by the rapid privatisation of the food industry. There is now no question of the fact that the user will determine what varieties should be grown. This must be deliberately put bluntly, because, in the final event, it is always the will of the user or customer that must be obeyed. The sugar industry (70,000-100,000 ha are sown to sugar beet each year in Hungary) does not use Hungarian varieties; the cultivation of foreign spring barley varieties is general for malt production; in the vegetable oil industry, too, foreign or joint Hungarian-foreign varieties are gaining more and more ground. This is dealt with in more detail below, when considering the situation in breeding research, but it should be mentioned here that only a complete production chain is capable of producing enough profit to finance breeding and research to ensure its own further development.

Institutional and Legal Aspects of Privatisation

The transformation of agriculture also caused serious problems in plant breeding R&D. The role of the state was reduced, leading to less support from the budget, and there was not sufficient capital in the background in Hungary to replace these losses. There is and was a law stating that growers must pay royalties to the variety owner for the seed they use, but due to the general agricultural crisis, the loss of foreign markets, the ground gained by foreign varieties and the teething problems of the new seed market, variety royalties were not able to make up for the deficiency. The breeding institutes were compelled to rationalise their activities, in some cases undertaking contractual work for seed companies and, most importantly, cooperating efficiently with organisations such as the Seed Product Council, which will be described below, in achieving an increase in the use of certified seed and in collecting seed royalties. Very little private capital is invested in breeding, and the private companies that carry out breeding are also engaged in seed production, processing and sales.

Specialists working in the seed sector soon recognised the need for associations to represent and protect their professional interests. This, too, rested on a long tradition, since the Association of Seed Merchants, which represented Hungary in the FIS, was founded as long ago as 1920. At the beginning of the political transformation, the Association of Hungarian Plant Breeders was reorganised and became a real professional forum. The responsibilities of the Hungarian Seed Product Council, set up in 1993 with 138 founder members, are determined by the law on agricultural regulation and by the interests of its members.

The Seed Product Council has members from throughout the seed production chain, from variety owners and breeders, through seed producers and processors, to seed merchants. The main responsibility of the Council is to reconcile interests and to regulate and coordinate the whole of the production chain in order to achieve the aim that the success of crop production should be ensured by the use of registered varieties and certified, dressed seed. In addition it provides professional advice and recommendations for the preparation of laws, decrees and standards connected with seed (the seed law, the decrees passed for its execution, the gene technology law, standards for field inspections and limit values, and any regulation brought by the customs office, the financial administration or the statistics bureau that has anything to do with seed).

In accordance with the Agriculture Regulation Law, the Seed Product Council has an obligation to cooperate with the Ministry of Agriculture and Rural Development, providing information on the seed sector, especially as regards the seed supply situation, and if necessary it reaches agreement with the Agricultural Minister on the regulation of the seed market. The Product Council is also responsible for gathering information for dissemination to its members. Soon after its establishment, the Product Council compiled and published a Seed Codex, which was a collection of all the laws, decrees, standards and regulations affecting seed, and a Code of Ethics to serve for the self-regulation of the market behaviour expected from members of the Product Council.

It should be emphasised that, in the market economy, the role of civil organisations, such as the Product Councils and professional associations, is of increasing importance. Due to the efforts of the Product Council, some of the subsidies available for crop production can only be granted if certified, dressed seed is sown. The Product Council now has almost 1000 members, representing some 95% of the seed-producing farmers.

Over the last five years, the significance of the Hungarian seed sector has perceptibly increased. Foreign seed companies, particularly the multinationals, but also smaller companies, have become more active. Hungary is now the third-largest exporter of seed to the European Union (Table 5). It is clear from the list of applications for state variety registration given in Table 6 that foreign varieties have gained considerable ground, especially for certain plant species. Ever greater importance is attached to seed quality, to the reliability of seed production (through the provision of irrigation facilities) and to quality guarantees.

Every seed production and supply system of the region originates from the traditional pattern that existed when the countries had centrally planned economies.

Table 5. Seed exports to the EU from various countries

Ranking	*Country*	*Value of seed exports (million ECU)*	%
1	USA	229 17	42.45
2	Canada	113 30	20.98
3	Hungary	32 88	6.09
4	Australia	20 92	3.87
5	Israel	13 76	2.55
6	Chile	13 33	2.47
7	New Zealand	11 64	2.16
8	Turkey	11 20	2.07
9	Japan	8 34	1.54
10	Mexico	8 16	1.51
11	China	7 22	1.34
12	Romania	6 78	1.26
13	Syria	4 83	0.89
14	Tanzania	4 78	0.89
15	Czech Republic	4 61	0.85
16	Poland	4 12	0.76
17	Ukraine	3 18	0.59
18	Switzerland	3 18	0.59
19	Croatia	2 07	0.38
20	Pakistan	1 87	0.35
-	Other	34 58	6.40
	Total	539 92	100.00

Today's differences between countries depend on how much progress each of them has made in the transition to a market economy and in diminishing the operating role of the public sector. Differences may be accentuated by the appearance of an informal seed supply system.

Table 6. Applications for state registration in Hungary

Year	Number of varieties			Ratio of Hungarian: Foreign
	Hungarian	Foreign	Total	
1970	203	9	212	96:4
1975	117	12	129	91:9
1980	163	19	182	90:10
1985	151	47	198	76:24
1990	194	116	310	63:37
1995	272	200	472	58:42
2000	165	385	550	30:70

Issues related to seed have in recent years become increasingly more complex. The reason is the involvement of more stakeholders: not only government policy-makers and public sector employees dealing with the seed sector, but also managers of seed companies, professionals in charge of research and plant breeding activities, marketing, trade and credit specialists, farmers, farmers' organisations and investors. The old issues have acquired a new relevance because the seed sector is competing with other economic sectors, and its future dimension depend on the level of efficiency and profitability it can achieve within the national and regional economies.

5

Seed Legislation and Regulatory Measures

The first seed laws that were enacted in most developing countries were based on the blueprint model supplied by the Seed Industry Development Programme of the FAO. The details depend to a large extent on the origin of the advisors assisting the development of the seed sector. India adopted a truth-in-labelling system of the USA, but combined this with a very strict variety control system from Europe.

The seed laws of many other countries simply took either the examples of France, Spain or UK as a basis, depending on their historical ties and official languages. While taking these European laws as a basis, they often picked the most stringent control mechanisms from these countries. For example the variety release system is based on government-run multi-location DUS and VCU tests whereas the marketing of certified seed of all crops is covered under comprehensive seed certification schemes. The level of regulation is commonly not in line with the level of institutional development of the country, leading to incomplete implementation and insufficient transparency. This creates a serious lack of credibility and inconsistent application of these regulations by the authorities.

Two rather opposite forces, globalisation and localisation, in development theory have inspired reforms to the standard regulatory systems. And both forces lead to calls for deregulation. Forces that relate to globalisation and liberalisation of markets oppose the existing regulations because the level of government control would hinder foreign investments in the seed sector and the emergence of domestic private seed enterprises.

Moreover, similar to the influence of past development assistance projects which advocated the establishment of public seed enterprises and their regulatory basis, recent projects put the needs of farmers' seed production, participatory plant breeding and establishment of small enterprise as the political and development agenda. This draws national and international NGO's into the policy debate and present a different role for seed quality assurance institutions. The belief that farmers' seed systems are important for on-farm management of genetic resources puts pressure to relax variety release procedures.

Liberalisation of trade requires the removal of obstacles by inefficient control agencies. The lifting of government controls may also assist the development of small seed enterprises especially where the inefficiencies of such institutions are translated into the certification and testing fees, and where market opportunities for local (non-released and possibly less uniform) varieties cannot be developed due to such restrictive seed laws.

The multinational seed companies that want to introduce varieties from their international breeding programmes and local seed enterprises and farmer-groups that may want to provide seed of locally adapted varieties (landraces) would benefit from lesser variety controls. Large seed companies may work with a (ISO) certification of their own internal quality control system. Small-scale seed providers would also better thrive on brand names than on government certification, especially where the regulatory institutions lack the capacity to check quite often remote seed production fields.

The options to reform these regulatory and institutional systems depend to a large extent on the existing institutions and organisations, on bureaucratic considerations, on regulatory cultures and international pressures. Deregulation has to strike a balance between the opportunities (promotion of private enterprise) and reduced consumer protection due to relaxed controls. Proposals to deregulate and change compulsory regulations into voluntary ones have to go hand in hand with educating the seed users where many farmers are unable to read seed labels. A truth-in-labelling system can very well be combined with prescribing certain minimum standards in order to reduce risks to farmers.

Deregulation Trends

Deregulation is a global trend in many sectors. The Sanitary and Phytosanitary Measures/Technical Barriers to Trade (SPS/TBT) agreement of WTO prescribes a framework for acceptable regulations for non-tariff trade barriers, which do not include extensive seed controls other than strictly necessary phytosanitary measures. There are, however, tendencies that go in opposite directions. These include particularly intellectual property rights, biosafety and access regulations on genetic resources.

First, the WTO-TRIPs agreement urges the development of plant variety protection laws in many developing countries. In contrast to conventional seed legislation that intend to abandon variety registration, the introduction of variety protection laws does require a detailed registration of the protected entity. Moreover, national and international seed trade will be influenced by protection claims, not so much because of government laws, but as the result of private law contracts and private market control organisations (e.g. ARPOV in Argentina) that regulate the seed trade.

Claiming intellectual property rights is a voluntary choice of breeders, but there is a trend that even public agencies are registering their varieties, either for profit or as a means to prevent others from claiming ownership. This new variety registration system will largely replace the 'old' variety release procedures and will curtail the use of 'protected' varieties in farmers' seed systems. This is exacerbated by the development of patent-protected transgenic crops.

Second, the introduction of transgenic crops forced countries to develop biosafety regulations that make the release of these varieties both for testing and for commercial use, dependent on extensive release procedures. In case the use of such varieties becomes more widespread, the reduction in variety registration procedures due to deregulation in conventional seed laws will be replaced by comprehensive release procedures under the biosafety laws.

Third, new developments within the framework of CBD may lead to even more variety regulatory systems than ever experienced under conventional seed laws. Access to genetic resources is made subject to national laws, based on Prior Informed Consent (PIC) and Mutually Agreed Terms that may have to be transferred from first user down the line, and which may lead to extensive variety regulations.

Seed Legislation and Regulatory Measures in the Near East North Africa

For centuries, farmers in the Near East and North Africa (NENA) countries have been selecting seed from their crops (cereals, vegetables, trees, etc), multiplying it, and sharing seed with their neighbours. Variety selection is primarily based on the level of plant adaptation to the prevailing harsh environmental conditions of the Region. In addition, farmers of the NENA region pay particular attention to culinary and other specific qualities of crops, which are seldom part of breeding objectives in modern variety development. As a result, farmers often complain about the taste of modern varieties when compared to their traditional landraces. Farmer preferences have contributed to the maintenance of most landraces and other varieties in the Region. For example, the durum wheat variety *Kyperounda* has been traditionally grown and maintained for decades in Cyprus and Morocco mainly due to the taste it produces in bread and pasta.

In the case of cowpea, farmers in the NENA region prefer traditional cowpea varieties compared to modern varieties. The traditional varieties are indeterminant, with longer growing seasons and maturity periods, while the modern varieties are determinant with short harvesting periods. Farmers prefer indeterminant landraces because of their extended harvesting period, which gives farmers the possibility to consume fresh pods and dry the surplus harvest for winter consumption. On the other hand, modern varieties mature simultaneously, which makes it possible to carry out mechanical harvesting.

In general, the exchange of seeds of improved field crop varieties by the international research centers including CIMMYT, ICARDA, CIAT, and CIP with national breeding programmes has been free if the seed is to be used for breeding and multiplication purposes. In an international trial conducted in several European countries by FAO and the Dorum Wheat Network, *Phibirol* a wheat variety that was selected in Cyprus by the author, was among the best performers. The government of Spain expressed interest in the variety and suggested to pay royalties. However, since the original material was received from CYMMYT free of charge, the author decided to turn down the offer and gave the variety *Phibirol* free to Spain. After further selection, the variety was released as *Karpasia* in Cyprus in 1984 and as *Sham 1* (*Waha*) in several other countries including Syria in 1984, Algeria in 1986, Saudi Arabia in 1987, Jordan in 1988, Turkey in 1990, Lebanon in 1994, and Sudan in 1997.

Need for Seed Legislation

Modern agricultural practices along with the establishment of the World Trade Organisation (WTO), and the Agreement on Trade-Related Aspects of Intellectual Property Rights (TRIPS) including Plant Breeders' Rights (PBR), have brought significant changes in plant breeding, seed multiplication and trade. The availability of seed of improved varieties at a reasonable price is a prerequisite for any significant progress in agriculture. Therefore, Governments and the private sector must be motivated to invest in highly trained staff and allocate essential resources in the seed supply sector. This can only be achieved, if varieties are registered and intellectual property rights are protected through proper legislation that cover seed trade within and between countries.

Present Situation of Seed Supply

Information regarding seed supply and legislation in NENA was obtained from various sources including FAO documents, country reports, regional meeting reports, and personal experiences. Seed legislation varies significantly within and between countries in NENA. However, seed laws and related regulations are only applied on the "Formal Seed Supply Systems", which cover only 10% of the seed needs of farmers. The remaining 90% of seed need is provided by the "Informal Seed Supply Systems", which are the exchange and sale of seeds from farmer to farmer.

Seed supply is well-developed in Morocco, Turkey, Pakistan, and some other countries that have established seed laws and seed certification systems. Seed quality control is essentially absent in Yemen, Qatar, Kuwait, Oman, and United Arab Emirates, which formally market a very small quantity of seed of the most important crops. Egypt, Jordan, Tunisia, and Syria are in the intermediate group of countries, with reasonably well-developed systems covering major crops.

Seed policies also vary among NENA countries. Morocco, Egypt, Tunisia, Ethiopia, Israel, Turkey and Cyprus have well-defined seed policies. For example, in late 1998 the Parliament of Cyprus approved a new seed law, which covers all aspects of seed production and importation. On the other hand, Iraq, Syria, Yemen, Libya and Jordan lack a defined seed policy, but have seed plans within their national agricultural policies. However, it is important to emphasise that existing seed laws do not apply to the Informal Seed Supply Sector.

Formal seed trade, for which seed laws apply, is controlled and subsidized by governments. Seed trade in the private sector is limited to a few countries and deals mainly with hybrid and vegetable seeds, and a few cereal seeds. Private seed companies operate in Tunisia, Morocco, Turkey, Jordan, Lebanon, Pakistan, and Sudan. In Cyprus, cereal seed trade is controlled by the government, but seed trade of potatoes, vegetables, pulses and forages is dominated by the private sector and co-operatives.

Seed legislation should be established to encourage the involvement of the private sector in seed supply and trade. It is also recommended that the subsidized government controlled activities are reduced to a minimum. In addition, the informal seed sector and its great contribution in the seed trade must be recognised and ways must be found to provide help in order to improve the quality of seed.

Imports and Exports of Seed of Improved Varieties

The climatic conditions in NENA countries characterised by limited precipitation are generally unfavourable for rainfed crops. Rainfed varieties are adapted to specific, but restricted locations throughout the region. As a result, there is a very limited seed trade of rainfed wheat, barley, and legume and forage crops. Import of seed for vegetable crops including potato, tomato, carrot, watermelon, and hybrid seed of corn, sugar beets, sunflower are common in almost all the countries.

Seed trade is generally controlled by local and foreign private companies and co-operatives. Most of the seeds imported by NENA countries come mainly from Europe. There are also very small seed import-export activities within the Region. Seed import regulations exist in Cyprus, Egypt, Tunisia, Sudan, Syria, Turkey, and Yemen. According to country laws, import of seed requires an import permit.

Intellectual Property Rights

It is widely accepted that "Plant Variety Protection" (PVP), which grants "Intellectual Property Rights" (IPR) to eligible plant varieties is essential to increase the availability of good quality seed of improved varieties. Breeding for high yielding varieties with all other desired characteristics requires considerable investments in trained staff and the allocation of funds.

If PVP is not granted, the private seed sector will not be willing to invest in plant breeding. At the same time, the availability of seed of improved and protected varieties at low prices in NENA countries and the granting of farmers' rights as defined in the FAO fora are issues to be considered when establishing PVP laws.

Most countries of the region have laws, which require that varieties should be registered to be released for commercialisation. However, many countries do not have legislation for PVP. In Cyprus, Egypt, Ethiopia, Lebanon, Libya, Morocco, Oman, Sudan, Syria and Tunisia, registration of varieties for commercial release is carried out through an independent body, by which governments control the evaluation of varieties according to the requirements established by the UPOV Convention, that is Distinctness, Uniformity and Stability (DUS).

Some of these countries carried out the Value for Cultivation and Use (VCU) test in addition to the DUS test. In other countries, the evaluation of varieties is conducted by a committee that also includes breeders. Plant Variety Protection does only require the DUS testing. Therefore, in such countries where the DUS testing is already functional for commercial listing, the implementation of PVP laws would not pose practical institutional problems.

In Cyprus, the release of varieties is based on trial results conducted by breeders and decided by a special government committee. Successful varieties are registered in the official commercial catalogue, and their seed is multiplied and marketed through the formal system.

Until recently, only Egypt had a law prepared for PVP. The reasons for limited efforts in PVP in the NENA countries related to several factors including the following.

Major breeding programmes have been carried out by government employees working in national research institutions or universities that did not seek any reward for their newly developed varieties. The great majority of seed (90%) is produced by the informal system, which makes it difficult to exercise Plant Breeders' Rights.

Local land varieties of the major cereal and legume crops whose breeders are unknown and, which are not eligible for PVP, are still grown. At a Plant Variety Protection workshop held in Cairo in 1999, it was indicated that many countries of the region are initiating procedures to develop legislation for the protection of Breeders' Rights.

Laws related to PVP are either in preparation or in parliament for approval in Cyprus, Egypt, Ethiopia, Iraq, Jordan, Lebanon, Mauritania, Morocco, Oman, Sudan, Syria, Tunisia, Turkey, and Yemen. In Morocco the law for PVP has been approved, but has not yet been put into practice.

Legislation for the commercial registration and protection of improved varieties are important to motivate scientists and attract private industries in plant variety development.

Effects of WTO's TRIPS Agreement on Plant Breeding, Variety Protection, and Seed Production and Trade

Several international organisations deal with plant variety protection and grant Plant Breeder's Rights. These organisations include the International Union for the Protection of New Varieties of Plants (UPOV), which is an independent intergovernmental organisation working in close collaboration with the World Intellectual Property Organisation (WIPO), and the International Association of Plant Breeders for the Protection of Plant Varieties (ASSINSEL).

The agreement on Trade-Related Aspects of Intellectual Property Rights (TRIPS) is one of the outcomes of the Uruguay Round Agreements under the World Trade Organisation (WTO). The TRIPS Agreement was established on January 1, 1995 and is considered the most remarkable multilateral agreement on intellectual property. In regard to plants, the TRIPS Agreement addresses issues related to intellectual property protection of plant varieties, requiring protection either by patents or by a sui generis effective system or by a combination of both.

As the Agreement does not define what would be considered a sui generis effective system, it will be for the TRIPS Council to judge. It is considered "effective" by the WTO. Developing member countries are given longer periods than other countries to develop their IPR legislation in compliance with the TRIPS Agreement (Article 65-4). Article 7 of the TRIPS Agreement, entitled Objectives, states: "the protection and enforcement of intellectual property rights should contribute to the technological innovation and to the transfer and dissemination of technology, to the mutual advantage of producers and users of technological knowledge and in a manner conducive to social and economic welfare and to a balance of rights and obligations".

The TRIPS Agreement also defines in detail national, civil and criminal procedures by which the rights of breeders are to be enforced. For example, it states that procedures must be fair and equitable, not unnecessarily complicated or costly, and should avoid time limits or unwarranted delays. The TRIPS agreement does not intend to restrict trade, but to encourage it in balance with the promotion of technological innovations.

Due to the benefits derived from protected varieties, it is believed that protected varieties are likely to be well-maintained and continue to produce quality seed that is representative of the original variety. As a result, farmers will have confidence in the genetic properties of the varieties, which could have a positive effect on the national, regional, and global seed trade. However, protected material is expected to cost more because of the loyalties that have to be paid to the breeder.

Plant Variety Protection and Conservation of PGR

As already mentioned, to be granted protection a variety must be new for not being previously commercialised before certain date and uniform and stable in its essential characteristics. PVP granted under the UPOV Convention provides exception for the breeder (the right to use the protected variety for further breeding without the authorisation of the breeder) and farmer's privilege (the right to keep seed from a protected variety for further replanting on farmer's own land).

The protection of breeders' rights can help to promote research programmes in the development of improved varieties. Enhanced breeding activities can increase the number of improved varieties under cultivation and promote plant genetic diversity across farmers' fields. For example, in Syria only two barley landraces, *Arabic Abiad* and *Arabic Aswad,* had been traditionally grown for decades.

Increased plant breeding activities also has direct effects on the conservation of plant genetic resources (PGR). Heitz stated that the main objective of plant breeders is not only to create new and uniform varieties, but also to maintain a large genepool to be used as a genetic reservoir for future breeding programmes. Therefore, the introduction of PVP legislation, which promote plant breeding activities, will help maintain the genetic diversity by:

Increasing Uniform Varieties

Increasing in the diversity of gene pools that are maintained by private breeders or public institutions for future breeding to meet competitions and challenges. FAO, IPGRI, ICARDA and other international or regional organisations are involved in collecting, documenting, conserving, utilising and exchanging PGR in the NENA region. The PGR of the NENA region must be made available to breeders or scientific researchers on mutually agreed terms. The PGR from the region should be studied, conserved, and better managed. This would facilitate the marketing of genes and generate financial benefits from breeders who develop commercial varieties from NENA's material.

The introduction of legislation on breeders' rights is a system that reward breeders for their innovative efforts. As it is often the case, plant breeders use in their breeding programmes the varieties that have been maintained by farmers; they improve these varieties and protect the new varieties, which are resold as seed to farmers. However, farmers, especially subsistence farmers, who have conserved the PGR of the region for generations.

As it is often the case, plant breeders use in their breeding programmes the varieties that are maintained by farmers; they modify these varieties and protect the new varieties, which are resold as seed to farmers. This was recognised as a problem by FAO member countries and the issue was addressed in the Resolutions 4/89 and 5/89 of Plant Genetic Resources for Food and Agriculture (PGRFA).

Farmers' Rights

Farmers' Rights were recognised and endorsed at a Conference in 1989 by FAO member countries in the International Undertaking on PGRFA. Farmers' Rights defined as the rights arising from the past, present and future contributions of farmers in conserving, improving, and making available plant genetic resources, particularly plants from the center of origin. Farmers' Rights are vested in the international community, as trustees for present and future generations of farmers, for the purpose of ensuring full benefits to farmers, and supporting the continuations of their contributions, as well as the attainment of the overall purposed of the International Undertaking. As a result, breeders' lines and farmers' varieties can be made available only with the agreement of individuals, communities, or institutions that developed or maintained the varieties.

A great part of improved varieties throughout the world were developed from materials collected from developing countries. Therefore, it appears important that developed countries assist in efforts to strengthen the capacity of developing countries to conserve, develop, and use their national plant genetic resources. In this regard, the establishment of a global fund was suggested at the 1991 FAO Conference on PGR in Rome. The resolution C5/91 gives details on the establishment of this International Fund for PGR in developing countries. However, no specific agreement on the nature and size of country contributions to the fund was reached.

The International Undertaking also recognises the sovereign rights of nations over their plant genetic resources. In this regard, at a South Asia-Southeast Asia and the Pacific meeting, it was proposed to establish an international taxation system on the sale of plant varieties and products of plant origins under the Intellectual Property System. The revenue collected through this tax system could be used to pay royalties to the country that provided the parent materials. However, the ways to implement this innovative idea are still a matter of discussion.

Most of the farmers in NENA are subsistence farmers who rely on their landraces of food legumes, forages and some cereal species for their livelihood. Therefore, seed legislation must provide adequate protection of Farmers' Rights for varieties that are used by breeders. In addition, any PVP law should include provisions to ensure the farmer's privilege at least to poor farmers in order to encourage farmers to continue participating in PGR conservation.

Plant Variety Protection Systems and Innovative Genetic Engineering Technology on Farmers' Variety Choice

The application of genetic engineering technology in plant breeding has recently increased in developed countries. Genetic engineering is slowly but steadily being applied in the NENA region. Clearly, substantial progress in plant adaptation to dryland areas and resistance to disease cannot be achieved by conventional breeding alone. Therefore, despite the negative public perception associated with biotechnology, genetic engineering technology will continue to be critical to the future development of new varieties in the NENA countries.

Varieties or landraces developed and maintained at high cost by breeders or farmers can be modified by genetic engineers at low cost. This can be accomplished by inserting one gene to produce an "essentially derived variety". The concept of essential derivation is related to the degree of similarity between the parent varieties and the derived variety. For the resulting variety to be "essential" there must be a high degree of similarity with one of the parents and a minimum number of characteristics (at most one) inherited from the second parent (if there is one). This facilitates an equitable share of benefits among holders of breeders' rights, and patent owners of the additional gene.

The provisions of the 1991 UPOV Convention offers a possibility to balance the rights of breeders of the "initial variety" and that of genetic engineers (patent owners). For example, the provisions extend breeders' rights from the "initial varieties" to the "derived variety" and breeder authorisation is needed in order to apply commercialise the derived variety. The advantage of this arrangement is that it promotes investments in classical breeding and discourages unfair or parasitical activities without discouraging genetic engineering application.

It is important that countries in the NENA region adapt these agreements to their specific conditions. By balancing the rights of conventional breeders, genetic engineers, and farmers, it is more likely that the availability of improved varieties will be increased and sustained.

Farmer's Access

The region shows a trend of a widening gap between production and consumption at a rate of 1% a year. This has made NENA the largest food-importing region in the developing world. Self-sufficiency and food security can be achieved by several measures including an increase in the availability of quality seed of improved and better performing varieties of food and feed crops at reasonable prices. This would require a strong and efficient seed supply sector.

The main advantages of improving the seed supply sector in the region include the following:

- Increase the availability at low cost of improved and adapted varieties that have the qualities preferred by farmers of NENA.
- Create a system for the multiplication and trade of seed according to international quality and phytosanitary standards.

Upgrading Breeding Capabilities

The development of genetically superior varieties is a prerequisite for future improvements of agriculture in the region. Currently, breeding programmes, especially for major food crops including wheat, barley, and legumes, are concentrated in government controlled institutions. The private sector involvement in plant breeding and seed production is limited and deal mainly with vegetables and hybrid seed. However, in the past 20-30 years, there has been a positive contribution by the CGIAR institutes including CIMMYT, ICARDA, IPGRI, CIAT, and IITA throughout the region. These institutions have upgraded the research and breeding capabilities in the region.

Breeding and seed supply activities can be enhanced if legislation on Intellectual Property Rights (PVP and patents) is introduced throughout the region. In this regard, private breeders and government institutions would be motivated to develop better varieties to compete in a free seed trade market. The economic incentives created through these new systems would make a positive contribution by promoting the use of more efficient breeding and screening methods suitable for the region and increase the adoption of new varieties by the farmers. Unsuitable material would be eliminated and breeders of this material would face economic failures. Profit-oriented breeding activities will generally utilise the most efficient methods including biotechnology to achieve goals faster, and will attempt to minimise costs. Under these conditions, the private sector would be expected to increase its share in breeding and government institutions and universities would have to upgrade their research and breeding capabilities to cope with the new conditions.

It is generally believed that the introducing breeders' rights and related legislation would have a negative impact on the protection of farmers' rights and conservation of plant genetic resources. Several countries in NENA have already started introducing legislation on the protection of varieties. Countries appear receptive to formulate concrete regulations based on the experience of Europe and other regions.

Seed Production and Trade

Currently, the seed trade of major cereals and legumes is government subsidised and controlled. The private sector handles mainly hybrid seed and other elite material. Seed trade is generally restricted to within-country exchanges of self-pollinated cereals and legumes, with only limited exchange of seed between countries in the region and with some European countries. The introduction of legislation on PVP and seed trade based on WTO agreements will improve the availability of quality seeds to farmers. In addition, enhancing and modernising breeding methods will increase the varieties of food crops with wider adaptation, and ultimately increase seed trade and availability of seed. The availability of hybrid seed would be improved if uniform legislation on seed trade is introduced in the region.

A combination of these factors would have a positive effect on good quality seed availability. By increasing the volume of seed traded in an open market, the cost of production to companies is expected to be reduced. The price of seed for subsistence farmers should also be reduced. As a result of growing better varieties, yields will be higher.

The Informal Seed Sector, which controls most of the seed trade of major food crops in the region is expected to be negatively affected as the role of the private sector expands. Assistance must be provided, especially on seed cleaning and seed health, to the informal seed sector in order to improve seed trade. Assistance should continue over the next 10-20 years as the informal seed sector is gradually transformed into a formal seed sector.

6

Seed Legislation and Regulation: A Global Scenario

Seed industry is crucial for modern agriculture, total sales and profits are not as large as for other agricultural inputs, such as pesticides, machinery or fertilisers. At the same time, countries need many large to small seed companies to ensure farmer access to a full range of technology from world and local research at competitive prices. With the modest total size of national seed markets on the one hand, and a need for many players on the other, a country's seed industry can be stunted or strangled if regulations are not workable.

Over the last decade, seed research, production and trade in Central and Eastern European Countries (CEEC), Commonwealth of Independent States (CIS) and other Countries in Transition (CT) have been moving from socialist patterns of organisation toward market patterns. Before 1990, regional agreements facilitated movement of varieties and seeds across regional borders. However, pre-1990 mechanisms for coordinating the seed industry have broken down, not only regionally but even within individual countries. Seed industries in many regional countries have suffered, losing access to new varieties from regional research on the one hand, and on the other losing access to regional markets.

In many countries, seed industries have turned inward, trying to survive on national research and protected domestic markets. Revising seed regulations has been and continues to be part of the process of ongoing changes in seed industries across the region. Unfortunately, many of the changes in seed regulations, as well as in seed production and trade, have been toward separate national markets and industries. Governments can foster a return to regional and international cooperation for their seed industries by: (i) harmonising seed regulations to world best practice; and (ii) further harmonising regulatory details and decisions according to regional agreements and practice.

Many regulatory features are crucial for the development of a market-oriented seed industry, including, for example, easy entry for new seed companies, allowing seed companies to contract with farmers of their choice, allowing seed companies to introduce new varieties, and giving seed companies responsibility and authority to ensure seed quality. In many countries in the region, local seed companies have a hard time doing their work because government licences and approvals are required at so many steps. In such cases, harmonisation to world best practice means an overall shift from ex ante controls on seed company business decisions and production processes, to ex post controls on truth-in-labelling at the retail level.

All of the countries in the region could have access to the best seed technology in the world at competitive prices by adjusting regulations to accept varieties and seeds from the EU, other OECD countries, and regional neighbours. This does not necessarily mean that foreign seed companies would invest or otherwise move in to take over markets. More often, regional and EU companies would seek partnerships with new or existing local companies to produce or market, or both, seeds of new varieties with features that farmers might want. In some cases, companies may want to move seed across borders to cut production costs and to reduce seed inventories.

Government control on the introduction of new varieties is a major obstacle in most countries. As far as the writer knows, Lithuania is the only country in the region that allows companies to introduce new varieties for all crops without government review (similar to USA, Malaysia, India, and many other countries). From 1997, Romania accepted all varieties from EU Common Catalogues without further in-country tests. Later, Bulgaria also took steps to accept varieties from EU Common Catalogues without further tests.

Recently, Albania has passed a new seed law that gives Albanian farmers access to new vegetable and flower varieties from all sources without prior government approvals. Another set of obstacles to seed industry development is in the controls that governments impose on seed company entry, seed farms and seed production. Most countries in the region have skilled technicians and farmers distributed throughout the country. Central controls on seed production, including compulsory certification and licensing for seed farms, can create conflicts with pro-market and pro-reform processes.

New seed companies coming out of old state seed companies and seed farms can find their hands tied at a time when they need to be able to act fast and on their own to adjust to market demands and opportunities. Overall, lack of harmonisation to international best practice regulations—especially using regulations to block new entry for companies and varieties—has delayed the development of mutually beneficial ties between national, regional and world seed markets. Only two regional countries, Hungary and Czech Republic, rank among the top 25 seed exporters.

Regional Harmonisation of Seed Regulations

Regional harmonisation of seed regulations is a concept that covers many options. In most discussions, the objective of regional harmonisation is to create a larger regional seed industry and market in place of multiple smaller national markets. With complete harmonisation, although that is not necessarily the intent of those who talk about harmonisation, companies would be able to operate across international borders within the region without any more effort than they face operating, for example, across oblast, state, or provincial boundaries in individual countries.

However, not all advocates for regional harmonisation want to go so far as to create one unified market. In some cases, objectives may be more limited. For example, countries might want to lower costs for registering plant variety protection (PVP), or they might want to improve phytosanitary controls against extra-regional pests. Below, some of the major issues and options for regional harmonisation of seed regulations are follows:

Variety Controls (i.e. allowing seed sale of a new variety)

In most CEEC, CIS, and CT, each governments decides what varieties seed companies are allowed to sell for most, if not all, crops, with government decisions based on government-supervised distinctness, uniformity, stability (DUS) and value in cultivation and use (VCU) tests. Options to harmonise variety controls across a region include:

— Each member government agrees to waive controls for some or all crops.

— For a list of crops, each country agrees to automatically accept varieties approved in any other country without further testing or decision. This is what is done in the EU.

— For a list of crops, countries agree to allow some regional body to test or to approve, or both, new varieties. This is what has been agreed among six Central American countries from early 2000. The arrangement is arguably unwieldy and unworkable. The governance of the regional body becomes an issue. Also, since it is a single body, it has monopoly authority (unlike the EU system, which lets companies choose which of 16 independent authorities to go through to get a variety approved).

Virtually all options to harmonise variety controls within the region offer far less benefit to a country than simply opening to varieties from all countries. Moreover, any country that accepts to work within a framework of regional variety controls may be binding itself into an agreement that blocks much greater potential benefits from unilateral opening.

For example, if Kyrgyzstan wants immediate access to new EU varieties, all it has to do is relax controls on variety introduction (e.g. no controls or automatic acceptance of varieties in EU Common Catalogues). If, however, Kyrgyzstan enters a regional agreement with four or five other Central Asian countries that includes controls on variety introduction, Kyrgyzstan, unless it withdraws from the regional agreement, no longer has the option to liberalise access to EU varieties.

Phytosanitary and other Import/export Controls

In many of the countries in the region, permits for seed export and import are not managed in a routine fashion. Phytosanitary controls are part, but not all, of the problem, since governments also control seed imports, and even exports, on the basis of other factors as well. Unlike variety controls, this is an area where farmers and seed companies in the region have something to gain from governments getting together. Through regional meetings, phytosanitary experts can pare the list of pests and diseases to control on seeds in regional trade to those that:

i) exist in some of the countries but not in others; and

ii) represent an economic threat.

When this is done, seeds for many crops can be moved from one country to another without phytosanitary certificates, while seed for other crops may be traded with phytosanitary controls for a reduced list of realistic threats. Another aspect of harmonising phytosanitary barriers can and should be to strengthen external barriers to a minimum standard. It is in the interests of all concerned that extra-regional seedborne pests and diseases do not enter any regional country.

Seed Quality Controls

This is another area where unilateral liberalisation is arguably more important than regional agreements to reduce obstacles to seed movement among countries. Options to liberalise or harmonise seed quality controls to facilitate regional seed trade include:

— The easiest solution is for regional countries to agree to allow commercial sale of truthfully labelled seed for most, if not all, crops.

— The next-easiest solution would be to agree to allow commercial sale of truthfully labelled seeds that meet minimum laboratory standards (germination and purity), allowing companies to do their own tests.

— Many countries in the region have mandatory certification for major, and even minor, crops. If countries in a regional agreement are not willing to give up compulsory certification for some crops, seed markets would be larger (and seed would tend to be cheaper) if countries would accept each other's certified seed. For several major crops, leading countries around the world already agree on certification standards through OECD Seed Schemes. Hence, those are the obvious standards for regional countries to endorse.

According to WTO, imports must be accorded equal treatment to locally produced goods. In other words, imported seed cannot be subject to more stringent quality controls than locally produced seeds. Many countries in the region are not members of WTO, so this condition does not constrain their actions. Nevertheless, this does show once again how de-regulating the internal market and harmonising to world best standards can eliminate many of the possible obstacles to regional seed movements.

Plant Variety Protection

In several regional agreements around the world, governments agree to recognise each other's decisions to assign PVP, and governments may create a regional body to assign PVP or patents.

Other Factors

Other minor details covered in regional agreements can include packaging, truth-in-labelling, tariffs, etc.

Harmonisation Strategies

Most of the interest in harmonisation flows from the gains that are expected with larger markets. Larger markets allow more (competing) seed companies to spend more to breed, test, and introduce new varieties. As already described, one way to move from a small national to a much larger regional or international seed market is to simply reduce barriers to varieties and seed moving into the country from other market(s). For example:

- — Australia links into the world seed market by allowing variety introduction from anywhere without government control. Phytosanitary controls on seed imports are science-based in theory (but may be excessive at times).
- — Romania and Bulgaria revised seed laws and regulations to allow automatic approval for all varieties in EU Common Catalogues. In the short time since Romania adopted this new policy, major European-based seed companies have established a presence in the market, companies have introduced many new varieties, and Romania's seed exports to the EU have boomed.

Another strategy for moving from smaller to larger seed markets it to harmonise regulations among countries in a region (Table 1). For example:

Table 1. Existing and prospective harmonised seed markets

Countries or Region	*Annual seed sales(US$ million)*	*Population (million)*
EU (15 countries)	5 500	350
Central America (Costa Rica, El Salvador, Guatemala Honduras, Nicaragua, Panama)	5	
MERCOSUR (Argentina, Bolivia, Brazil, Chile, Paraguay, Uruguay)	2,500	400
Malawi, Mozambique, Zambia, Zimbabwe	85	60
Kenya, Tanzania, Uganda	35	80

— The EU is the oldest and best example of countries harmonising seed regulations to facilitate variety and seed movement. Varieties and seeds move across the EU with little regard for borders. Within the EU, we can see some specialisation among countries in seed production. For example, France produces about 80% of EU maize seed, while the Netherlands produces over two-thirds of EU potato seed. However, across all crops, national seed production tends to follow national seed sales. For example, French seed imports are less than 20% of total seed sales (domestic and exports), while seed exports account for about 25% of total sales.

— From early 2000, agriculture ministers from six Central American countries—Costa Rica, El Salvador, Guatemala, Honduras, Nicaragua and Panama—agreed to adjust regulations to create a regional seed market for five crops: rice, field beans, soybean, maize and sorghum. Ministers

not only country-by-country, but also considering several countries together, to allow world class research and competition to develop without at the same time taking steps to allow closer ties with the world seed market and industry.

For each country entering a regional agreement, the gains (and losses) that are possible depend on: its pre-existing degree of openness; whether the proposed regional market is open or closed; the size of the country; and the size of the proposed regional market. The interplay of some of these issues is illustrated in Table 2. In most cases, the dominating feature is openness.

Table 2. Potential gains to farmers, seed industries and seed companies in shifting from national to regional markets

Country considering joining a regional market	*Characteristics of the proposed regional market*	
	Closed regional market	*Open regional market*
Closed country	Minor to medium positive impact if the new market is very large (>US$ 1 million/yr)	Large positive impact:- Farmers see more varieties and competition.- National seed industry expands.- Individual companies may suffer.
Open country	Large negative impact:- Farmers see fewer varieties and less competition.- National seed industry loses partners and markets.	Minor positive impact, since farmers, seed industry, and seed companies are already working with the world seed industry.

While farmers, consumers, and agri-businesses will almost invariably gain from access to more (foreign) varieties and seed companies, local breeders (in the public sector) and seed companies may fear losses from competition. Since there are many more farmers than public breeders, there should be no choice between giving farmers access to the best seed vs protecting government breeders. In practice, one of the best investments during transition may be to support public breeding and research from the government budget so that they do not oppose liberalisation of variety introduction, which would allow farmers to buy seeds of better foreign varieties.

Role of Government and Private Sectors

Although governments may take the initiative during periods of major change or reform to draft new seed laws and regulations, achieving workable regulations over time almost always requires dialogue with a private seed industry. It is not easy, in other words, to draft workable seed legislation unless one can see how the private industry is working. Furthermore, seed regulations are never a finished business. As technology and other factors change over time, the regulatory needs adjustment. For example, a decade ago there was little discussion about how to regulate agricultural biotechnology. Similarly, before the Trade-Related Aspects of Intellectual Rights (TRIPS) agreement in the mid-1990s, there was little interest in many countries to protect intellectual property rights in varieties.

What this means in practice is that seed legislation is a work in progress, and this is especially so for many of the countries in the region, where competitive private seed industries are still emerging from state-managed trade and research, and in some cases with excessive controls on entry, production and trade. Although most of the countries in the region passed new seed legislation in the 1990s, often with technical assistance provided by the EU, World Bank, FAO or other aid agencies, many of these laws and supportive regulations are less than ideal and will be amended and even replaced over time as countries continue to move towards private seed industries and competitive markets well linked to the world seed industry.

If things are working as they should, multiple domestic groups of seed experts contribute to regulatory design over time. These include the local private industry (seed companies and association[s]), public breeders, and regulators. In addition, politicians ideally represent the interests of broader groups in the society. In some situations, what seed companies, breeders and regulators want may be damaging to farmers, consumers and agri-businesses. For example, regulators may want more authority and higher fees.

Private companies and public breeders may want protective tariffs or other barriers against foreign seed and varieties. Hence, as seed regulations evolve over time, it is up to politicians to represent the interests of farmers, consumers and agri-businesses wishing for access to the world's best varieties at a price that is not unnecessarily inflated by regulatory costs and restricted competition.

International Assistance

The prospects for harmonisation to have a beneficial impact on farmers and seed industries in the region can be broken down into several subregions.

(i) For the 10 countries in Central Europe that plan to join the EU in the near to intermediate future, harmonisation for all intents and purposes means opening to the EU and to the world seed industry and markets. These 10 countries represent some of the strongest seed industries in the region. Seed companies in Poland (US$ 400 million annual sales), Hungary (US$ 200 million annual sales), and Czech Republic (US$ 150 million annual sales) already have many joint ventures with EU and other foreign companies, and are getting tied into world research and trade. Romania and Bulgaria have unilaterally accepted varieties in the EU Common Catalogue. At the same time, in the short term, all 10 countries could gain from more open and liberal regulations facilitating closer ties with non-EU companies.

(ii) Newly independent countries in south Central Asia have at least informally considered the option to harmonise seed regulations. The gains that are possible for any such regional grouping are probably too small to bring them together. Large gains in access to new varieties, competitive seed markets and seed export sales are not possible for these countries without also including Russia, but, even so, bigger gains are possible by simply liberalising to work with EU and other OECD seed companies, as well as with Russia and other regional countries.

(iii) Yugoslavia's break up leaves a number of neighbouring countries with small seed markets, but with good research and technical skills. All regional countries have more to gain by harmonising to EU and world markets than by any attempt to work back into a closed but unified regional market. Furthermore, if everyone opens to world markets, they will also be opening to each other, which may be the easiest way to recover some of the gains from regional trade and cooperation.

(iv) Newly independent countries in the Caucasus are countries that also have small markets. The best options may be to work more closely with Russia, the EU and other OECD countries. By far the biggest gains come with opening to OECD seed companies and markets, with or without enhanced trade and exchange among regional countries.

(v) Among Russia, Ukraine and other countries in Central Europe, Russia and Ukraine have been regional leaders in research and seed trade. Maintaining this position depends at least in part on continued excellence in research. This is only possible with active private as well as public scientific partnerships and exchange with OECD universities, research organisations and companies. Over time, as competitive seed industries develop in the region, countries that have been leaders in the past can be expected to maintain strong positions in regional markets on the basis of their large size, as well as continuing scientific leadership. For Russia and Ukraine, opening to western companies and markets is crucial to maintain regional leadership.

Although harmonisation to world best practice is the most important task, within subregions there are opportunities to cut costs and to improve efficiency through regional cooperation, particularly in the areas of PVP and phytosanitary controls.

Role of International Organisations

Through the 1990s and ongoing, bilateral and multilateral donors and other foreign and international organisations have often advised and otherwise pushed countries in the region to adjust seed regulations and seed industry organisations. After 10 years, it can be seen that some things have worked, but many have not.

Arguably, the international organisations that have had the most favourable impact are the public and private organisations that focus exclusively on seed issues, including Union Internationale pour la Protection des Obtentions Vegetales (UPOV), FAO's Interim Commission on Phytosanitary Measures, the International Seed Testing Association (ISTA), OECD Seed Schemes, and FIS (Federation Internationale du Commerce des Semences). The influence that these organisations have grows over time as more regional countries become members and as seed trade, seed companies and national associations emerge and grow. So far, 22 regional countries are members of ISTA, and 11 are members of UPOV. Five countries (Czech Republic, Hungary, Russia, Slovakia and Slovenia) have seed associations that are members of FIS.

In addition to the activities of these seed-specific organisations, many bilateral donors and international organisations—including the EU, World Bank, FAO, USAID and others—have sought to influence seed sector development through technical assistance, grants and loans. After 10 years, success has often been partial or absent. Looking to the future, we can reasonably expect that technical assistance and aid will continue to many countries in the region. The impact of this aid might be improved with attention to some of the following issues.

First, development of national seed industries in isolation is not a reasonable goal. One of the major challenges is to encourage international openness and partnerships—be it in public research, regulatory design, private joint ventures, or whatever—so that ambitions and skills that are currently under-used and frustrated in countries with stagnant and isolated seed sectors are given an opportunity to contribute as much as they can.

Second, in all OECD countries, seed regulations—in practice, whatever the details and differences might be in design—allow competitive markets. OECD countries allow new entry for small to large companies, foreign and local companies, and new varieties. Too often over the last decade, donors have advised and helped regional governments to design and implement new seed regulations that are technically accurate and superficially similar to what is done in one or more OECD countries, but which are in practice an obstacle to new entry and competition.

For example, donors have advised and assisted many countries in the region to establish centralised seed certification agencies. In some cases, ministries are using (or threatening to use) these new centralised agencies to control who can produce seed, obstructing local initiative (including local organisations that have many years of experience producing high quality seed). In most OECD countries, certification is either voluntary or decentralised (in the EU, to member governments), so that the centralised seed regulatory organisations that aid has helped to build are arguably not standard practice across OECD countries.

Finally, as private seed industries develop in regional countries, it gets easier over time for technical assistance to work not only with government agencies but also with the private sector. As the private seed sector develops, special attention should be given to small and medium enterprises and retail sales. Wherever these can develop, large seed companies will also have opportunities. In contrast, if local small and medium enterprises are not able to get into the seed business, many foreign companies with useful varieties will not be able to find local partners, and large companies that are already in the market may have trouble getting their seeds to farmers (for lack of retail outlets). Regulations that work for small and medium businesses will work also for large companies, but it is small businesses, and new entry, that are crucial for seed industry development over time.

Divisions in Seed Market

There are some clear divisions within the seed market, which profoundly affect the organisation of seed supply. One is the volume and value of the seed, both in themselves and in relation to the crops which they produce; this determines the extent to which it is possible to make a viable business from producing and selling seed, in other words, the potential to support a "commercial seed market." In general, crops such as cereals, with high sowing rates and relatively low crop values, are difficult to commercialise, while those such as vegetables, with low sowing rates and high output values, can command a good market price and support a commercial seed trade. Therefore the ratios of volume, value and output potential are major factors in determining how the seed trade works, and it is segmented into different crop groups. Crops such as sugar beet and some forages also have good commercial potential because of the technical difficulty of producing the seed.

A further consequence of this is the partition of the seed supply between formal and informal channels, as represented in Figure 1. This reflects the fact that in most crops, seeds can be produced by the farmers themselves and there is no obligation to purchase each year. Collectively, we may speak of the "seed supply system" to mean the complete mix of formal and informal channels by which farmers satisfy their total seed requirement each year.

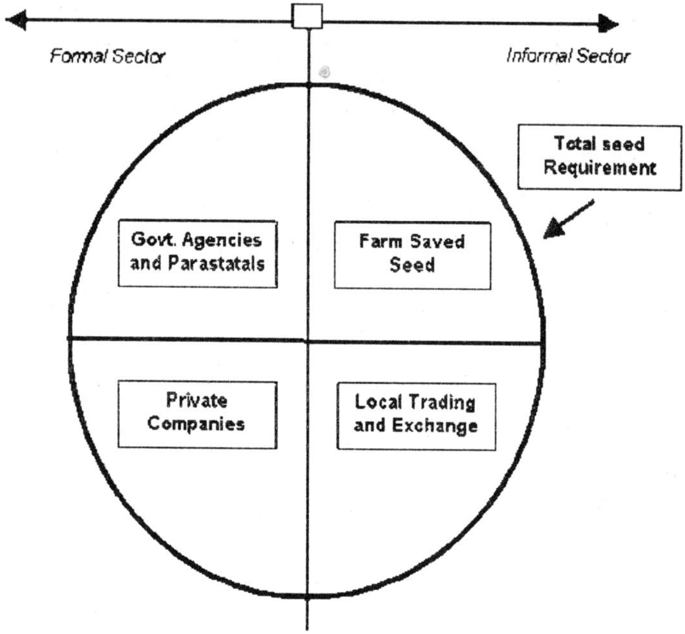

Figure 1. Components of the seed supply system

However, the actual partition varies widely between different crops and countries, depending on the economic circumstances. The term "seed industry" refers to the organised formal sector, which has local, national, and—in some crops—global dimensions. In contrast, the informal seed system is normally localised at the farm or community level and has relatively little organisation.

Previous Seed Supply System

The essential characteristics of the previous seed system were its independence from market considerations and its emphasis on total control, regardless of cost. Being geared in most countries to the needs of large state farms, this meant very high volumes, in terms of both production quantity and quality control. However, this seed system was not entirely separate from grain production: grain crops were inspected and could continue to be used for seed if necessary, while seed crops could be diverted to grain use if the overall seed need was satisfied. This was a very elaborate system, but it was an integral part of the central planning process for agriculture and so cost implications and market considerations did not apply. As a result, the informal sector, which is the default supplier of low-cost seed in most other countries, simply did not exist because the entire seed supply system was administered by the Ministry.

The structure of agriculture has changed and the resources are no longer available to run a system of that size. It is therefore necessary to find new ways to organise seed supply, both in terms of production and quality control. This is now a matter of some urgency in many countries, following a decade of deterioration in the state system, with virtually no investment made. One major question is: How to create new viable enterprises in the vacuum created by the near-collapse of the old system? In the past, there was no diversity, no competition between suppliers and no product identity, except for the variety name. This has left a very strong legacy, as there is no experience of, and in general no facilities for, relatively small-scale seed supply. The only model is the large-scale one, which is unsustainable on cost grounds in a market-oriented economy.

Problems of Re-structuring the Seed Sector

The general context of re-structuring throughout the region is the need to introduce a financially self-sustaining seed supply system. In view of the constraints on government funding due to limited budgets, this implies an increasing role for the private sector in production. However, problems of terminology may arise here. For example, in some countries, former state farms have been privatised in name, but their mode of operation may have changed little: they are still very large production units, and perhaps in some areas they will remain the main viable unit for crops such as cereals. Nevertheless, there is a need to plan for a more diverse structure in agriculture, both in terms of the production units themselves and the organisations that service them, even if this process moves slowly in some countries.

Consequently, there are two distinct aspects of re-structuring. First is the 'internal' re-organisation of the components of seed supply, such as production, processing, storage and distribution. The second is the ongoing change in the structure of the agricultural sector itself, as the user of the seed. This is important because the trend towards smaller private farms requires a completely different marketing and distribution strategy to that which existed before. There may be a need for packing in smaller units, wider distribution and more active contact with customers, all of which contrast with the former system in which seed, like other inputs and equipment, was simply 'allocated.' The immediate problem is the acute lack of experience in carrying out such market-oriented tasks.

A further dimension, particularly in the countries of the former Soviet Union, is that agricultural production did not take account of self-sufficiency on a 'national' basis. For example, while wheat was the staple food in the region, in some countries the supply of grain came mostly from other republics of the Union. This has had a profound effect in some countries, which, following political and economic independence, have felt the need to produce more wheat, and perhaps other crops, to reduce dependence on imports.

This changes the overall cropping pattern and may lead to a seed demand that did not exist before. There may be other effects of the collapse of this integrated economic system. For example, Kyrgyzstan was formerly a livestock-producing country, with huge, intensive units, but the market for their output has disappeared, leading to a dramatic reduction in the livestock population and in the demand for fodder crops.

Despite the importance of seed in agricultural production, they alone cannot change fundamental structural problems in the sector. For example, in some Central Asian countries, the rural economy is seriously lacking financial liquidity, because of the bankruptcy of many old institutions. This makes it very difficult to re-establish a "normal" commercial trading system for buying and selling seed, or any other commodities. The barter system that has developed as a substitute is very inefficient in comparison with cash transactions. It is therefore essential to have a realistic view of what the seed sector can contribute to reviving agriculture. Seed can certainly make a vital contribution, but alone cannot transform a rural economy subject to many other constraints. Seed must be considered in the wider context of agricultural input supply and output marketing, of which it is an integral part.

Regional Differences and Groupings

This meeting has brought together a very wide range of countries, united solely by their recent history of a socialist economic system, in which state farms and cooperatives were the main organisational unit of agricultural production. There are, however, some clear geographical groupings within the countries represented here. The countries of the former 'Eastern Europe' and the Baltic States are looking westwards to the EU, with a view to membership in the short to medium term. Their guiding principle, therefore, is how to integrate into a larger Europe. The Caucasus countries, by reason of their position and small size, have strong links to Russia and—in some cases—also south towards Iran.

The Central Asian Republics form another large group, with links to Russia, but perhaps more southwards to Pakistan and the Indian subcontinent, and to Turkey for ethnic reasons. The old 'Cold War frontiers' imposed barriers that had no relation to agro-ecology, and Central Asian Republics' complex boundaries that were largely irrelevant within the Soviet Union are now real national frontiers. Consequently, there are strong regional dimensions in planning seed sector development. It is important to expand regional trade wherever opportunities exist, while at the same time ensuring that countries do not create new barriers 'accidentally' by introducing divergent regulations and policies. That is perhaps the most important objective of this meeting.

7

Farm Legislation Issues in Cotton

Cotton is the single most important textile fiber in the world, accounting for 40 percent of all fibers produced. Cotton is an enormously important commodity throughout the world. However, many farmers in developing countries receive a low price for their produce, or find it difficult to compete with developed countries.

This has led to an international dispute:

> On 27 September 2002 Brazil requested consultations with the US regarding prohibited and actionable subsidies provided to US producers, users and/or exporters of upland cotton, as well as legislation, regulations, statutory instruments and amendments thereto providing such subsidies (including export credits), grants, and any other assistance to the US producers, users and exporters of upland cotton.
>
> On 8 September 2004, the Panel Report recommended that the United States "withdraw" export credit guarantees and payments to domestic user and exporters, and "take appropriate steps to remove the adverse effects or withdraw" the mandatory price-contingent subsidy measures. The international production and trade situation has led to 'fair trade'

cotton clothing or footwear (Veja Sneakers) being available in some countries. The fair trade system was initiated in 2005 with producers from Cameroon, Mali and Senegal.

On average, the United States produces an estimated 20 percent of global cotton production, accounts for more than 10 percent of world cotton use, and is the leading supplier in the international market. The U.S. cotton industry generates more than 400,000 jobs among the various sectors from farm to textile mill and accounts for over $25 billion in products and services annually.

Cotton is produced in 17 southern U.S. States-from Virginia to California-with major concentrations on the Texas Plains, in the Mississippi, Arkansas, and Louisiana Delta, California's San Joaquin Valley, central Arizona, and southern Georgia. The predominant type of cotton grown in the United States is known as American upland-which accounts for about 97 percent of U.S. production-with the balance commonly referred to as American Pima or extralong staple (ELS). ELS cotton is produced chiefly in California, with small amounts also grown in southwest Texas, New Mexico, and Arizona, where it is well adapted to the arid conditions.

According to the 1997 Census of Agriculture, about 31,500 farms in the United States grew cotton, compared compared with 43,000 farms just a decade earlier. The trend to fewer but larger cotton farms has increased the average size by nearly 200 acres since 1987 to 420 acres of cotton per farm in 1997, the largest of any major field crop. As a result, an increasing share of U.S. cotton is produced on 500-acre or larger farms. In 1987, this category represented only 12 percent of the farms and less than half the production. By 1997, however, the 500-acre or larger farms accounted for 29 percent of all cotton farms and contributed 71 percent of U.S. production.

Cotton acreage in the United States rose modestly during the 1990s, averaging about 14 million acres. During this time, area expansion-once a westward shift-returned to the eastern half of the Cotton Belt. Significant gains occurred in the Southeast, where cotton acreage more than doubled over the past decade. Factors contributing to the reversal included the success of the boll weevil eradication programme in the Southeast, making cotton more profitable, and water limitations in the West related to drought conditions. In addition, planting flexibility under the 1996 farm legislation permits producers to change their enterprise mix to maximise net returns.

Benefits from the cotton marketing loan programme have also kept cotton production attractive relative to competing crops such as soybeans, corn, or sorghum. In 2000, the lack of profitable alternatives pushed cotton area above 15 million acres for only the second time since the early 1960s. And, cotton area will remain above this mark for a second consecutive season as plantings of nearly 16.3 million acres were estimated for 2001. Key producing States and their percent of U.S. planted acreage for 2001 include: Texas (38 percent), Mississippi and Georgia (10 percent each), and Arkansas and North Carolina (7 percent each).

Biotechnology has also become an important factor in cotton production. Since their introduction in 1996, biotech cotton varieties (Bt and herbicide-tolerant crops) have been adopted rapidly by U.S. farmers seeking to reduce pest management costs. In 2001, adoption of biotech cotton increased to 69 percent of the acreage planted to cotton, up from 61 percent in 2000. While government programmes and prices of cotton and competing crops have influenced acreage, weather has been the chief determinant of yield variability. Since 1991, U.S. cotton yields have averaged nearly 645 pounds per harvested acre but have ranged from a record 708 pounds in 1994 to 537 pounds in 1995.

During the past 3 years, however, cotton yields have remained below the average, and concerns about the focus of cottonseed breeding programmes have developed. During the past decade, production has varied from a record 19.7 million bales (1 bale = 480 pounds) in 1994 to only 13.9 million in 1998. In 2000/01, the United States produced an estimated 17.2 million bales of cotton, the most in 3 years. And, if average conditions are seen in 2001, U.S. cotton production is likely to exceed last season's crop at a time when demand has been dampened by the recent economic slowdown in many countries around the world.

Demand and Textile Trade

Cotton demand fluctuates annually and depends heavily on the strength of world economic conditions. Over the past decade, domestic mill use accounted for 60 percent of the total disappearance of U.S. cotton, while exports accounted for the remainder. However, exports are becoming more important as restructuring in the U.S. textile industry-due to lower trade barriers and lower labor costs outside the United States-limits mill use. U.S. cotton mill use climbed steadily throughout much of the 1990s as consumer demand increased for natural fiber clothing, like denim.

U.S. mill use peaked in 1997/98 at a near-record 11.3 million bales. However, competition from less expensive apparel imports-exacerbated by recent trade agreements and a strong dollar-has reduced domestic mill use since then, forcing some industry participants to limit output, relocate, or close operations. With the continued liberalisation of world textile and apparel trade, the U.S. cotton textile trade deficit (imports less exports of semi-processed and processed products) continues to expand.

The North American Free Trade Agreement (NAFTA)-which became effective in 1994-along with the Caribbean Basin Initiative (CBI) accelerated the growth of U.S. cotton textile and apparel imports, which have seen significant gains over the last decade. In 2000, U.S. cotton textile and apparel imports rose for the 12th consecutive year, while exports improved for the 16th straight year. Also in calendar year 2000, the raw-fiber equivalent of cotton textile and apparel imports exceeded the quantity of cotton used by U.S. mills for the third consecutive consecutive year. At the same time, however, more U.S. cotton is contained in these imported products than ever before, due largely to NAFTA and CBI. These agreements have provided a "home" for U.S. raw cotton and semi-processed cotton products used in apparel manufacturing, an outlet that might otherwise have been unavailable. This trend is likely to continue into the foreseeable future.

The United States, the largest cotton exporter in the world, has accounted for a 25-percent share of global cotton trade over the last 10 years despite profound changes occurring in the world cotton market. These changes involve global cotton consumption and its increasing concentration in a handful of producing countries, altering U.S. export destinations. Over the past decade, the leading markets for U.S. cotton have changed from China and Japan to Mexico and Turkey. In 2000/01, the United States exported an estimated 6.6 million bales of cotton-a 25-percent share of world trade-with nearly 30 percent of the total destined for Mexico.

Global Cotton Economy

As the global cotton economy enters the first decade of the 2000s, global consumption of cotton is again trending upwards. The 1990s saw stagnation in world cotton consumption as the Soviet Union's textile industry collapsed, polyester consumption soared in the late 1990s, and the Asian financial crisis sent a shock wave through the Asian-dominated textile industry. The 1990s were a period of stagnation for consumption in China and Pakistan, in particular, the two leading sources of increased consumption during the 1980s.

China and Pakistan again led the world in the consumption rebound during the last 2 years. Furthermore, polyester consumption gains have slowed, cotton/polyester price ratios have returned to more average levels, and the longrun deterioration of cotton's share of world fiber consumption has slowed. Cotton consumption is growing in Russia, but even after 2 years of growth (through 2000/01), consumption is still expected to be 85 percent below its 1989/90 peak. Similarly, the transformation of South Korea, Taiwan, and Hong Kong into middle-income Newly Industrialised Countries (NICs) and the expansion of world trade in apparel have led to a continued decline in textile consumption of cotton fiber in the NICs, Japan, and the European Union (EU).

As a group, these countries' share of world consumption during 1999/2000 and 2000/01 is estimated at 10 per-cent, compared with 16 percent 10 years earlier. This trend predates the 1990s, and reflects the growing importance of lower-income countries in the production of apparel and, more recently, textiles. Debt problems and economic contraction throughout much of the developing world during the 1980s in part led India and much of

Latin America to abandon the constraints that previously oriented their economies away from trade. The 1990s saw the results of this policy transformation, and India's cotton consumption soared as domestic economic growth and textile exports responded positively.

India's cotton consumption rose 4.9 million bales during the 1990s (56 percent), and production rose 1.6 million. In contrast with India, liberalisation in Latin America meant that many countries that formerly protected cotton growers from competition removed those barriers, and production fell despite rising consumption. Latin America's production fell as much as 3.2 million bales during the 1990s, even as consumption rose 2.5 million. More recently, the phenomenal potential of Brazil's Mato Grosso has helped Latin America's cotton output increase 1 million bales, although the region remained a net importer for the 9th consecutive year.

Liberalisation in Central Asia has been much more limited, but cotton production has fallen 5.6 million bales since the region's independence from the Soviet Union. The limited nature of economic reform in Uzbekistan and Turkmenistan is arguably one reason cotton production and exports are falling: state marketing orders and monopolisation of foreign trade have been used to transfer resources from agriculture to industry, including textile production. Environmental damage and food security concerns also helped cut area devoted to cotton in the region by about 30 percent since the late 1980s. While reduced, the region's exports are still second only to those of the United States, and WTO membership is a distant prospect for all but a few of the smaller republics.

In contrast, area has been rising in the Franc Zone countries of West Africa since the CFA Franc's devaluation in 1994, and both West Africa's and

Australia's cotton area has been trending upwards for decades. Neither exporter consumes a significant portion of their production, although Sub-Saharan Africa holds perhaps the world's greatest untapped potential for apparel production. For the foreseeable future, institutional issues-like the ongoing privatisation of the Franc Zone's cotton-trading parastatals-and restoration of civic and economic infrastructure in a number of formerly large cotton producers in the region remain unresolved.

Finally, China's sheer size and volatility affect every aspect of the world cotton sector, and are likely to do so for the foreseeable future. China, the world's largest producer and consumer of cotton, is believed to hold about 30 percent of world stocks and is the largest exporter of garments in the world. China's cotton production fluctuated substantially during the 1990s as the adjustment of government-set purchasing prices failed to keep pace with changes in agriculture and the economy. China's cotton area, imports, ending stocks, and exports ebbed and flowed as China's policymakers lowered and raised procurement prices, opened and closed import quotas, and offered and withdrew export subsidies. China was at times the world's largest importer (1994/95-1996/97), but in 1998/99 was the world's fourth-largest exporter.

During 1999/2000, China finally extended to its cotton producers limited rights to sell cotton to buyers other than the government's Cotton and Jute Bureau, and withdrew from attempts to fix domestic cotton prices. These changes came more than a decade after similar reforms for grains and oilseeds, and the impact on China's cotton sector remains unclear as cotton area first fell and then rebounded as the government auctioned millions of bales from old-crop stocks. With China's agreed: (i) to accept common certification standards; (ii) to streamline phytosanitary controls to focus on science-based concerns; (iii) to introduce PVP; and (iv) to cooperate to approve new varieties for seed sale in all five countries, based on regional tests.

— A number of seed harmonisation schemes are under discussion, including six countries in MERCOSUR, four in southern Africa, and the three in eastern Africa (Table 2).

Benefits from regional agreements may be obscured if we focus too much on the EU. Because the EU market is so large, it is easy to overlook the high degree of openness between the EU and the rest of the world. Without access to non-EU technology and markets, EU seed companies could not and would not compete on a world scale. Even for the EU, with its enormous market, liberalisation is more important than harmonisation.

If we look outside the EU, harmonisation to world best standards becomes even more important. Consider, for example, the new regional seed market that has been created among six small countries in Central America, with estimated annual sales of US$ 5 million. With a market that is so small, it is more important for seed companies that they can move varieties and seeds into or out of the region (e.g. from Mexico or Brazil to Panama) than from one small intra-regional market to another (e.g. from Panama to Nicaragua).

In countries with small seed markets, the option to form small to medium regional seed markets offers little gain unless there is first harmonisation and liberalisation to world best practice. This is the situation that applies to most CEEC, CIS and CT. Seed markets are far too small, accession to the WTO, a TRQ that grows to 4.1 million bales by 2004 will be implemented, with an in-quota tariff of 1 percent.

Costs and Returns

The financial viability of U.S. cotton farms varies greatly depending on costs of production, yield, the type of farm, prices, and other factors. Costs of producing U.S. cotton climbed steadily throughout much of the 1990s, largely the result of increased costs of fertilisers and chemicals. Cash receipts for cotton and cottonseed have not kept pace with the cost of production, however. During the 1991-99 period, the farm value of cotton did not cover all production costs, with the exception of the 1994 and 1997 crops. Returns from cotton production peaked in 1997 but have dropped significantly since then to their lowest level during the 1990s. Consequently, government payments have been critical for cotton producers to show a profit during the past decade and particularly in the last several years.

Based on data from USDA's 1997 Agricultural Resource Management Study (ARMS survey), total economic costs for all cotton farms in 1997 averaged 73 cents per pound, with operating costs averaging 38 cents per pound. Based on the cumulative distribution of total costs, only 45 percent of the cotton farms, accounting for 62 percent of production in 1997, were at or below 73 cents per pound. On average, all cotton farms in 1997 provided a return above total costs of $42 per planted acre. However, returns can vary significantly depending on farm characteristics. In 1997, based on the ARMS survey, operating costs ranged from 35 cents per pound of lint production for farms with low sales (sales below $100,000) to 40 cents for other small farms-those reporting major occupation other than farming, retired, or limited resources-and non-family farms.

When total costs were examined, costs ranged from 68 cents per pound for non-family farms to 80 cents for farms with high sales (sales between $100,000 and $250,000). While returns adequately covered operating costs for all categories, returns above total costs showed a different picture. Returns above total costs were generally low or negative except for the nonfamily and very large family (sales above $500,000) farm types. U.S. upland cotton farm prices have varied significantly over the past decade, ranging from a high of over 75 cents per pound in 1995/96 to a low of 45 cents in 1999/2000.

The upland cotton loan rate has remained constant since 1995/96 at 51.92 cents per pound, the maximum established in the 1996 farm legislation. Like farm prices, the variable cost of cotton production has varied, ranging from 38 cents per pound in 1992/93 to 56 cents in 1995/96-a year of low yields resulting from major pest damage. And, with the recent rise in energy costs, variable expenses are likely to rise in 2001/02. Since 1995/96, the farm price and the world price for upland cotton (AWP)-which is used to determine if some programme benefits are applicable -followed a similar pattern. The AWP fell below the loan rate during 1998/99 and triggered programme payments to cotton producers that have provided a significant portion of their income in recent years.

Government Programmes

U.S. farm policy affects the cotton market as well as producers' incomes. Many cotton producers benefit from the production flexibility contract (PFC) programme, the commodity loan programme, subsidized crop and revenue insurance, and market loss assistance. Cotton producers may also benefit indirectly from programmes that increase cotton use through promotion and trade liberalisation. Total planting flexibility, introduced in the 1996 Farm Act, enabled many cotton producers who had participated in previous commodity programmes to shift production to other crops such as corn or soybeans, while permitting producers of other crops to shift area to cotton without sacrificing programme benefits.

In 1996, approximately 16.2 million acres of cotton (99 percent of eligible acres) were enrolled in the programme. For the 1996-2002 crops, producers who participate in the PFC programme receive payments that are not linked to current production or prices-also known as "decoupled" payments. The 1996 Farm Act appropriated a fixed amount of money to be allocated among participating producers each year. In addition, Congress authorised supplemental payments for the 1998-2000 crop years-known as market loss assistance (MLA) payments-as a result of low prices and severe weather. These payments made to eligible participants were proportional to the PFC payments, approximately 50 percent for 1998 and 100 percent for 1999 and 2000.

Like the PFC programme, the MLA payments are not linked to current prices, production, or resource use. As such, these payments, like the PFC payments, go to those holding cotton contract acreage and not necessarily to current cotton producers. Another key policy tool for cotton producers is the marketing loan programme to assist farmers when market prices are low. The programme provides producers a combination of commodity loan programme benefits and direct payments that guarantee a per-pound revenue floor. Nonrecourse loans are available to eligible cotton producers who pledge their production as collateral. These loans may be repaid through forfeiture of the cotton to the Commodity Credit Corporation (CCC) at maturity without penalty or they may be repaid at the current repayment rate-the lesser of the loan rate plus interest or the AWP-at or before maturity. When the AWP for upland cotton falls below the loan rate, loan deficiency payments (LDPs) or marketing loan gains (MLGs) are triggered and available to eligible producers.

From the 1994/95 season through most of 1997/98, the AWP was above the loan rate and no LDPs or MLGs were made. However, world prices have fallen since then and remain below the loan rate, triggering these benefits. During the 1999 crop year, upland cotton producers benefited significantly, receiving about $700 million in loan deficiency payments and more than $800 million in marketing loan gains. As a result of relatively low prices, these marketing loan programme payments equaled about 40 percent of the 1999 market value for cotton.

Cotton producers also benefit from the U.S. crop and revenue insurance programmes to guard against adverse weather, insect infestations, and other natural perils. USDA pays a portion of the contract premiums for producers' insurance policies and also pays some of the delivery and administrative costs of private insurance companies that handle policy sales. During the 1999 crop year, 90 percent (13.4 million acres) of the cotton area was covered by insurance, with participation concentrated in the High Plains of Texas and along the Mississippi Delta. Texas, Georgia, and Mississippi accounted for over 65 percent of the insured area.

Special programme provisions also aim to keep U.S. cotton competitive on the world market. These competitiveness provisions are known as Step 1, Step 2, and Step 3.

Step 1 allows for a further reduction in the upland cotton loan repayment rate. An adjustment may be made by the Secretary of Agriculture when the AWP is less than 115 percent of the upland cotton loan rate and the lowest U.S. Northern Europe price quotation exceeds the Northern Europe price quotation.

Step 2 is used chiefly to promote the use of U.S. cotton and is accomplished through the issuance of Step 2 payments to exporters and domestic mill users of U.S. upland cotton. These payments are issued in a week following a consecutive 4-week period in which the lowest U.S. Northern Europe price quotation exceeds the Northern Europe price quotation by more than 1.25 cents per pound. In addition, the AWP cannot exceed 134 percent of the U.S. loan rate. If these specified conditions are met, payments are made to domestic mill users on documented raw cotton consumption and to U.S. exporters on documented export shipments. Since the mid-1990s, approximately 60 percent of these payments have gone to domestic mill users. A similar competitiveness programme is also available for ELS cotton.

Step 3 permits special import quotas for upland cotton. A quota is announced if, for any consecutive 4-week period, the lowest U.S. Northern Europe price quotation (adjusted for any Step 2 value in effect, unless U.S. supplies are extremely tight) exceeds the Northern Europe price quotation by more than 1.25 cents per pound. The quota equals 1 week's domestic mill use of upland cotton at the seasonally adjusted average rate during the most recent 3 months for which data are available. However, an import limitation of 5 weeks' consumption is based on the first quota established in the marketing year.

The form in which government payments and other benefits are provided to the cotton sector is important because of the obligations of the United States under the Uruguay Round Agreement on Agriculture (URAA). The total amount of support from all U.S. programmes of certain types is limited to a specified maximum amount under the URAA ($19.1 billion in 2000). The covered programmes are those considered to have the most potential for production and trade distortion, and are called "amber box" programmes.

Examples of these programmes for cotton producers include the loan deficiency payments, marketing loan gains, and other benefits related to the commodity loan programme. In these cases, the amount of benefits for a producer of cotton depends on the current level of production and the current market price of cotton relative to the announced loan rate. Although the insurance programmes are considered amber box programmes, they are implemented using non-commodity-specific (generic) provisions.

As a result, they would count toward the U.S. upper limit on agricultural support only if the total benefits from all non-commodity specific amber programmes exceed 5 percent of the total value of agricultural production in the United States (the de minimis provision), something that has not yet happened. On the other hand, "green box" programmes are those considered to have the least potential for production and trade distortion.

Benefits from these programmes do not count toward the limits on total U.S. support levels. Examples include environmental, conservation, and resource retirement programme payments in which producers agree to use certain production or conservation practices. The Conservation Reserve Programme is included here. The PFC payments to cotton producers are also considered to be green box because the payments are "decoupled" and were predetermined by the 1996 farm legislation.

In contrast, while MLA payments-like PFC payments -are also based on past production and resource use, the MLA payments were legislated annually in response to recent market price declines. Consequently, the MLA payments may be assumed to be related to market prices after the PFC (or WTO) base period, making them ineligible for green box programmes. As a result, the United States has notified the WTO that crop MLA payments mandated by recent emergency legislation are non-product-specific amber box payments.

Policy Choices

The current farm economy environment is much different today than during the farm bill debates leading up to the passage of the 1996 farm legislation. For the cotton industry in the early 1990s, U.S. cotton stocks were relatively tight, as a robust demand environment had developed. As a result, nominal farm prices for cotton were rising and had reached their highest level in over a decade. In contrast, the current environment includes very low commodity prices, rapidly rising costs, and strong international competition.

While some of the same concerns-like planting flexibility -will be addressed in this farm bill debate, the challenge for the next farm legislation will be to provide a better safety net for farmers that is budget-driven, environmentally responsible, enhances market access, and is within the guidelines of U.S. trade commitments.

Historically, ideas fall into one of three views on policy choices. One view favors a combination of support programmes wth no supply controls; the second favors supply controls; and the third view favors a more market-oriented policy.

Support Programmes

Continuation of traditional support programmes includes the Agricultural Market Transition Act (AMTA) payments or PFC payments. Planting flexibility, as introduced by the 1996 farm legislation, is also considered to be a vital component of the next farm bill. Allowing producers the option to change their enterprise mix from year to year to maximise net returns is seen as one of the successes of the current legislation. For upland cotton, planting flexibility has provided area ranging from 13.1 to 16.1 million acres since 1996. However, falling farm prices over this period have left producers' incomes vulnerable as AMTA payments are fixed and not related to current production or prices.

As a result, there is additional support for a stronger "safety net" programme that provides supplemental income to producers to help offset crop revenue shortfalls due to poor yields and/or low market prices. This countercyclical support would preempt the need for the ad hoc emergency assistance provided over the last several years. A criticism of the PFC programme's fixed payments has been the inadequate response during times of greatest need. Countercyclical payments, on the other hand, would be based on the difference between some current measure and a trigger level during a reference period. Some proposed triggers include farm income, gross revenue, gross returns, or gross cash receipts.

Traditional support also includes maintaining the current marketing loan programme with slight adjustments. This includes adjustment to the commodity loan rates to rebalance price relationships among covered crops. Also, elimination of payment limitations under the marketing loan programme is advocated by some.

Supply Controls. A second view, which was quite popular from the 1930s to the early 1990s, recommends adoption of supply control programmes to manage surpluses. However, supply controls overlook the response of foreign producers to expand output when U.S. prices rise, requiring tighter restrictions to maintain farm price levels. Imports have accounted for a larger proportion of U.S. mill use during the 1990s, and the growing need for reciprocal market access suggests U.S. imports should remain at least as open, and that imports will rise with U.S. prices.

In addition, higher priced U.S. crops are likely to lose additional export market share, as in 1998 when the U.S. share of world trade plunged to 18 percent from 28 percent the year before. Australia's, Franc Zone Africa's, and Brazil's Mato Grosso cotton area have tended to increase steadily during the 1990s, and could expand even more rapidly if unilateral reductions in U.S. production support world prices.

Market-Oriented Policy

The more market-oriented view recommends ending the decoupled PFC payments and opposes countercyclical payments, arguing that they would be reflected in land prices and rents, forcing farm operations to grow larger to cover the increased costs. This view suggests that, instead of income support programmes, similar funding be used for new programmes focusing on risk management, trade expansion, rural development, and technical assistance to small farms.

Despite the wide range of differences on programme direction, there is agreement on some issues. These include improved access to foreign markets and the exclusion of food from unilateral sanctions. In addition, proposals have been made for increased research in numerous areas, including biotechnology, food safety, disease prevention, and environmental quality. Also, there is a recognised need for programmes to assist farmers in meeting conservation goals and environmental mandates. Recommendations include increased technical assistance, cost-share programmes, and incentive payments for use of environmentally friendly practices.

WTO Issues

New multilateral trade negotiations under the World Trade Organisation (WTO) were initiated for agriculture in 2000. International trade is particularly important for cotton, since 30 percent of the world's consumption of cotton fiber crosses international borders before consumption by textile mills, and, through trade in yarn, fabric, and clothing, much of the world's cotton crosses international borders at least once more before reaching its final consumers.

While export subsidies for cotton by WTO signatories have been negligible, and market access liberal, government policies governing the role of State Trading Enterprises (STEs) and support of local textile industries have affected cotton trade. While textile trade rules are not a subject of the current negotiations, they are an important multilateral trade issue affecting cotton, and significant changes in textile import barriers are mandated by 2005, under the Agreement on Textiles and Clothing (ATC).

The removal of these import barriers could increase the vulnerability of both Mexico and the United States to apparel competition from outside of North America, slowing the integration of North America's textile industry, and diverting more U.S. cotton to other destinations. Other WTO issues related to cotton trade include China's accession, the accession of Central Asian cotton exporters such as Uzbekistan, the role of STEs in these and other countries, and domestic support for agriculture.

Significant domestic support for cotton production is provided in the EU as well as the United States. Domestic support programmes affecting cotton are also in place in China, Turkey, Egypt, Brazil, and Mexico. However, except in the EU and China, the level of assistance these foreign countries provide to cotton producers is low. Domestic support provided by developed countries is a concern of many developing countries.

For example, the EU notified the WTO of payments supporting cotton totaling 809 million ECU in 1997/98, an amount comparable to the value of the entire crop. Restrictions on market access for raw cotton around the world have traditionally been limited, since importers were generally countries lacking the natural resource endowments necessary to grow cotton.

Thus, the most commonly applied tariff level is 0 percent. Similarly, non-tariff barriers to cotton by major importers are uncommon, and there have been few instances of tariff-rate quota creation since the signing of the URAA: only by the United States, South Africa, and Colombia. Generally, cotton-producing countries have higher than average tariffs and account for most of the high bound tariffs and all the TRQs.

Cotton producers are increasingly importing, so market access is increasingly important to world cotton trade. In 1989, 12 percent of world cotton trade was imported by countries producing more than half of their cotton needs, and by 1999 this share had risen to 25 percent-a total that rises to 33 percent if former large producers like Mexico are included.

8

Farm Legislation Issues in Soybeans

The soybean is the world's foremost provider of protein and oil. The soybean plant is a legume related to clover, peas and alfalfa. Soybeans, similar to maize and sugar beats, are planted in late spring and flower in the summer. These flowers produce 60-80 pods, each holding three pea-sized beans. The crop is then harvested in early fall.

The history of soybeans can be traced to China where as early as 5,000 years ago, Chinese farmers grew soybeans. Soybeans history in the US; however, is relatively recent. The US involvement with soybeans is believed to be dated back to 1804, when a Yankee clipper ship brought soybeans to the US. The ship was loaded with soybeans because while leaving China, sailors loaded the ship with soybeans as an inexpensive ballast. Upon the ships arrival in the US the sailors dumped the soybeans to make room for cargo.

Soybeans are the second-highest valued crop in the United States, trailing only corn. The farm value of soybean production in crop year 2000 was $13.1 billion. More than 80 percent of U.S. soybean acreage is concentrated in the upper Midwest, although the historically important areas of the Delta and Southeast still account for a significant share. Soybean acreage in the South has declined steadily since its peak in the 1980s because yield growth there has lagged that of other areas. In the United States, soybeans are most commonly grown in a crop rotation with corn and other grains. Double-cropping of soybeans with winter wheat occurs mostly in the South.

New seed varieties, more effective fertiliser and pesticide applications, and improved management practices have caused yields to rise, thereby encouraging expansion of soybean acreage. Higher yields reduce perbushel costs of production, which enhances profitability. U.S. average soybean production costs were $249 per acre ($6.23 per bushel) in 1999. Operational costs (including seed, fertilisers, chemicals, fuels, and hired labor) averaged $76 per acre ($1.91 per bushel). Allocated overhead (such as land cost, capital recovery of machinery, and taxes) averaged $173 per acre, but tends to be lower for the largest farms because it is distributed over more output.

Thus, while nearly all soybean farmers can cover their annual operating costs at current prices, some smaller farms may have trouble paying off debt on fixed investment and securing a reasonable return on their own labor and management. Midwestern soybean producers generally have higher yields and lower per-acre cash costs than southern and eastern producers.

In recent years, soybean farmers have increasingly adopted conservation tillage practices to reduce production costs, help protect soil and water resources, and provide other environmental benefits. More than 45 percent of U.S. soybean acres are conservationtilled. After

1985, many producers adopted conservation tillage to meet conservation compliance requirements that were enacted in farm legislation. Higher yields from improved retention of soil moisture also contributed to the trend toward conservation tillage.

Tillage systems can also influence input use. With less soil cultivation, weed control depends more heavily on herbicide applications. Pesticide use (nearly all herbicides) on soybeans ranks second only to corn. In 1997, commercial fertiliser was applied to less than 40 percent of soybean acreage, a much lower rate than for most row crops (e.g., corn and cotton). Unlike other major crops, soybeans can fix their own nitrogen and require minimal nitrogen fertiliser. Irrigation was used on 4.2 million acres of soybeans in 1997, or 6 percent of total acreage. Most of the irrigated soybean acres are in Arkansas and Nebraska.

Herbicide-tolerant soybeans were among the first bioengineered crops to achieve commercial importance. Since their general commercial introduction in 1996, herbicide-tolerant soybean varieties have gained rapid acceptance among U.S. farmers seeking reduced costs and a simpler method of pest management. In 2001, these varieties account for 68 percent of U.S. soybean planted acreage. Farm acreage surveys indicate that soybeans account for most biotech crop acres, followed by corn and cotton. The popularity of bioengineered soybeans with U.S. farmers has ramifications for resource use, marketing, and international trade.

Farmers adopting herbicide-tolerant varieties of soybeans have reduced the number of per-acre herbicide treatments and tend to use herbicides with less toxicity. Bioengineering of oilseed crop traits initially focused on improving production attributes, such as lower pest control costs. But development of soybeans with enhanced functionality characteristics-such as healthier oil attributes, improved animal nutrition, and more palatable food quality-is progressing.

Whether U.S. farmers will continue to expand their use of biotech seed depends, in part, on the acceptance of biotech crops in domestic and foreign markets. Farmers in Argentina and Canada are growing biotech crops as well. Some governments, such as the European Union and Japan, require labeling of foods containing biotech ingredients, and other countries are considering similar labeling policies. There is also some debate regarding whether to segregate biotech and non-biotech crops in the marketing chain. Segregation of non-biotech soybeans would add to producers' and grain handlers' costs, but consumers' willingness to pay premiums necessary to cover these costs is uncertain.

Farm Structure

Census of Agriculture data indicate that 354,692 U.S. farms raised soybeans in 1997, down from 511,000 in 1982. With more acreage and fewer farms, harvested soybean acreage per farm increased from 114 acres in 1978 to 186 acres in 1997. While 77 percent of the farms growing soybeans were small farms (less than 250 acres), these farms accounted for only 34 percent of 1997 soybean production. Individual or family farms accounted for 82 percent of farms producing soybeans and 71 percent of soybean production in 1997. Partnerships and small family-held corporations accounted for much of the remainder, while other corporations produced only 0.4 percent of the total soybean crop. Tenant farmers accounted for 17 percent of U.S. soybean production, full owners produced 15 percent, and part owners produced the rest.

Domestic Use

Domestically, nearly all soybeans are processed (crushed) to extract the oil for food and industrial use and the high-protein meal for animal feed. A comparatively small amount of whole soybeans is used for seed, on-farm dairy feed, and direct food uses such as tofu. Soybean crushing operations are generally located near major soybean production regions, with easy access to rail and barge carriers that transport products to domestic feed markets and to export markets via ports located on the Gulf of Mexico.

Soybean meal is the most valuable valuable product obtained from soybean processing, ranging from 50 to 75 percent of total value (depending on relative prices of soybean oil and meal). Soybean meal is the world's dominant high-protein feed, accounting for nearly 65 percent of world supplies. Livestock feed accounts for 98 percent of soybean meal consumption. The remainder is used in human foods such as bakery ingredients and meat substitutes.

Soybean oil's contribution to soybean value is smaller, as it constitutes just 18-19 percent of the soybean's weight. Yet soybean oil accounts for about two-thirds of the vegetable oils and animal fats consumed in the United States. It is used mainly in salad and cooking oil, bakery shortening, and margarine, but also has a number of industrial applications. Worldwide, soybean oil is the largest source of vegetable oil, but palm oil, whose use has grown rapidly, looks likely to displace soybean oil's top ranking within a few years.

Trade and Trade Agreements

The world oilseed market consists of many closely substitutable commodities, such as soybeans, rapeseed, sunflowerseed, and cottonseed. Exporting countries also process oilseeds domestically and ship the resulting protein meal and vegetable oils to foreign buyers. Foreign import demand depends on the deficit between countries' domestic oilseed output and their consumption. Relative demand for protein meal and vegetable oil, and limits on domestic processing capacity, determine the ratio of oilseeds and oilseed products that countries will import.

The volume and source of for-eign imports depend on seasonal availability and relative prices, credit and delivery terms, local preferences, and quality. Importing countries' policies, such as tariffs and domestic subsidies, also can influence shipments by adjusting local prices and the availability of competing products. Since the oil content of soybeans is relatively low compared with other oilseeds, the dominance of soybean oil in the world vegetable oil market has waned.

The United States is the world's largest exporter of soybeans, and exports represent a significant source of demand for U.S. producers. Among all U.S. agricultural products, only feed and food grains together outrank the oilseed sector in total export value and net exports. For the 1999/2000 marketing year, exports of soybeans and soybean products accounted for 40 percent of U.S. soybean production, and were valued at $6.6 billion.

For the United States, major export destinations for whole soybeans include the European Union (EU), Japan, Mexico, China, and Taiwan. Important markets for U.S. soybean meal exports include the Philippines, Canada, Saudi Arabia, Venezuela, and Turkey. With so much competition from other oils, U.S. soybean oil exports are widely dispersed and are heavily influenced by concessional food aid to developing nations under the P.L. 480 food aid programme. U.S. imports of oilseeds and products amounted to $1.9 billion in 1999/2000, mainly rapeseed and rapeseed products from Canada, olive oil from Western Europe, and tropical oils from the Philippines, Indonesia, and Malaysia. USDA administers two credit guarantee programmes that help finance a portion of U.S. oilseed and oilseed product exports.

The Export Credit Guarantee Programme (GSM-102) and the Intermediate Export Credit Guarantee Programme (GSM-103) are used to underwrite credit extended by U.S. banks to approved foreign banks to pay for food and agricultural products sold to foreign buyers. In essence, the credit programmes assure U.S. exporters that they will be paid for their products. Following the Asian financial crisis of the late 1990s, credit became particularly important in supporting U.S. agricultural exports to several countries. Multilateral negotiations to discipline the use of export credits for all nations are ongoing.

Another programme, the Foreign Market Development Programme (FMD) uses funds from the USDA's Commodity Credit Corporation to aid in the creation, expansion, and maintenance of foreign markets for U.S. agricultural products, including oilseeds and products. World trade in whole oilseeds, particularly soybeans, is relatively unrestricted by tariffs and other border measures. However, to help protect domestic oilseed processors, many countries place higher tariffs on oilseed meals and vegetable oils, in particular, than on oilseeds. For example, applied tariffs on soybean oil average about 20 percent among the world's top consumers and importers of the commodity, compared with rates generally at or below 10 percent for soybeans.

Western agricultural interests and processors have sought for many years a worldwide elimination of all export subsidies on oilseeds and their products in exchange for abolishing import tariffs on them. The U.S. share of global exports has steadily diminished in the past two decades despite substantial growth in U.S. soybean output and recent gains in export volume. In the mid- to late 1970s, the United States dominated world trade in unprocessed oilseeds, with a market share of more than 70 percent. Recently, this share has fallen below 50 percent. The United States has seen its share of soybean meal and soybean oil exports fall even more sharply, although from a smaller base, particularly before 1990. One reason U.S. soybean meal exports have experienced a relative decline is the recent expansion of U.S. meat exports, which has raised domestic meal use rather than contributing to exports of soybeans or soybean meal.

A particularly important factor in the declining share of U.S. exports has been the phenomenal growth of foreign soybean output and exports, particularly by Brazil and Argentina. Foreign soybean output now exceeds that of the United States, and Brazil and Argentina share approximately a third of the soybean export market, up from less than 15 percent before 1980. With increased production, and more rapid expansion of trade in soy products than in whole beans, Brazil and Argentina have each overtaken the United States in soybean meal and soybean oil exports. Soybean production in South America has expanded rapidly since the early 1970s.

Brazil is now second to the United States in soybean production. Major Brazilian soybean-growing regions were formerly concentrated in the south, relatively near the principal ports. In recent years, soybeans have expanded into the vast farmland of the center-west States, as infrastructure improvements have cut internal transportation costs. Brazil's vast reserves of farmland will permit significant expansion in soybean area once prices strengthen. Argentina's soybean-growing regions and crushing mills are located close to port facilities, and the relatively small domestic market makes it the world's largest exporter of soybean meal and oil. Brazilian and Argentine soybean and meal exports are projected to capture market share from the United States in the next decade.

China is the world's fourth-largest producer of soybeans. Major Chinese soybean-growing regions are concentrated in the country's northeast. Yet rapid growth of China's economy has spurred food consumption, turning the country into a leading soybean importer. More growth is likely, as China's per-capita consumption of meat and oils is still well below developed-nation levels. Changes in China's agricultural and trade policies have greatly influenced world oilseed markets. The anticipated accession by China to the World Trade Organisation will reduce import barriers on vegetable oil. Once a WTO member, China is likely to experience lower internal oil prices and profit margins for oilseed crushing as a result of sharply higher oil imports, which would in turn favor imports of oilseed meal over oilseeds.

The European Union is self sufficient in vegetable oil production, but its protein meal deficit still makes it the world's largest import market for soybeans and soybean meal. Since the 1960s, EU imports of soybeans swelled because of rapid growth in livestock production and duty-free concessions signed in world trade agreements. But in the 1970s and 1980s, consumption slowed and EU agricultural policies subsidized a large expansion in domestically produced rapeseed and sunflowerseed, which eroded the market for foreign oilseed imports. The U.S. government challenged these subsidies, and in 1992 the EU committed to reforms of its Common Agricultural Policy (CAP), including area limits on the planting of oilseeds.

Following further reforms of the CAP, low prices have prompted EU farmers to scale back oilseeds planting recently. Within 3 years, direct payments to oilseed producers will be incrementally reduced by a third (to equal the payment that grains producers receive), which could further discourage EU oilseed production. Historically high import tariffs on cereals had boosted EU consumption of soybean meal, which has been favored by duty-free access for soybeans. But in coming years, EU grain supplies are projected to swell and the CAP reforms will allow EU grain price supports to fall even more. Despite very low meal prices, the reduction in the relative cost of feeding grains should cut EU soybean meal consumption and imports in the future. The relative weakness of European currencies against the U.S. dollar has also deterred imports of soybeans and soybean meal.

Under NAFTA, Mexico reduced its soybean import tariff from 15 percent to 10 percent in 1994, and will phase it out completely by 2003. With reforms in domestic crop support programmes, imports have virtually displaced domestic soybean production in Mexico, with nearly all of the imports coming from the United States. Since 1993, U.S. soybean exports to Mexico have doubled. Strong income growth in Mexico's economy has boosted consumption of meat and vegetable oil, which consequently raised soybean processing. Improvements in Mexico's rail links at the border have also expedited soybean trade.

Prices and Farm Returns

In spite of several years of relatively high prices, U.S.

soybean acreage stagnated in the 1980s largely due to farm programme features for other crops. At that time, farmers were reluctant to risk future government payments on programme crops (such as corn and wheat) for any temporary advantage in planting soybeans. Deficiency payments were paid based on historical plantings and yields of specific crops, which did not include soybeans and minor oilseeds. In fact, when other grain crops were in oversupply and the government implemented its acreage reduction programmes for them, quite often soybean plantings would slip as farmers would preserve their programme base acreage.

Soybean prices were higher because of this programme distortion, which encouraged expansion of acreage in South America. In the 1990s, U.S. farm legislation was reformed to promote greater planting flexibility, making expected market returns the major determinant of farmers' cropping patterns. Nearly all supply controls on U.S. field crop production (which were tied to deficiency payments) were eliminated in 1996. Now, when prices increase because of rising world consumption consumption or smaller harvests by export competitors, U.S. producers can respond by planting more soybeans.

Consequently, U.S. soybean acreage has increased each year since 1992, in part because of comparatively favorable market returns during the early and mid-1990s. Much of the expansion occurred in traditional wheat-producing areas. Steadily rising yields, a greater number of half-corn/half-soybean rotations, and low production costs (partly due to widespread adoption of herbicide-tolerant varieties) have also favored expansion of soybean acreage. Despite the lowest market prices since 1972, U.S. farmers planted a record 75.4 million acres of soybeans in 2001, which is a third higher than the 1990 acreage. Much higher per-acre costs to fertilise corn also discouraged some corn planting in favor of soybeans.

While planting flexibility has been successful in expanding soybean acreage when prices are rising, a contraction in acreage when prices fall has been less forthcoming. A major factor inhibiting a cut in U.S. soybean area is the marketing assistance loan programme, which was first instituted for soybeans in 1991 but has become relevant only with the low prices of the last 3 years. USDA announces a national average loan rate each year prior to planting and determines county loan rates available to oilseed farmers. The marketing loan provides benefits or direct payments (loan deficiency payments or LDPs) to cover the difference between the market-clearing price and the announced commodity loan rate whenever the price falls below the loan rate.

Farmers are guaranteed a per-bushel revenue floor regardless of how low market prices fall. Many farmers have even been able to achieve per bushel returns somewhat above the loan rate, by timing their LDP when cash prices are the lowest relative to the loan rate and then selling the crop later at a higher price. Although market prices are not supported, LDPs and marketing loan gains became particularly important in providing income support following sharp price declines in crop years 1999 and 2000, when soybean producers received $2.3 billion and $2.4 billion, respectively. Thus, U.S. farmers have been insulated from falling market prices and have had little incentive to scale back soybean planting.

With low prices encouraging higher consumption, U.S. exports and domestic use of soybeans have surged to record volumes, but increases in demand have not been enough to keep prices from falling further. Not all of the price pressure is entirely due to U.S. supplies. Very low costs of production and currency devaluation in Brazil have allowed South American farmers to resist reductions in soybean planting. In fact, with the very high yields of the last 3 years, South American soybean production expanded nearly 20 percent. World soybean stocks have accumulated since 1998, when a sharp decline in Asian economies curbed demand. World demand has subsequently rebounded, but the growth in output has temporarily outpaced growth in consumption.

Policy Choices

Marketing Loan Programme

The marketing loan programme would be retained under many proposals, with some changes. Some advocate a change in the current eligibility for locking in an LDP after harvest to any time after planting, which could allow some producers more flexibility to maximise their payment when prices are seasonally higher. To lower the comparative returns for soybeans to a more historic level, many proposals would raise loan rates for other crops relative to the soybean loan rate. Currently, the loan rate formula is not in effect as the Secretary of Agriculture has used authority to maintain the loan rate at the statutory maximum of $5.26. This effectively keeps more acreage in soybeans, as the loan rate formula would have reduced the loan rate to $5.17 in 2000 and to the $4.92 minimum in 2001.

One plan would retain this authority, but change the current law's minimum loan rate of $4.92 per bushel to $5.26. As under current law, if prices eventually increase, the loan rate would adjust upward to 85 percent of the season average price for the previous 5 years (excluding the high and low prices). If higher loan rates for other crops succeed in reducing soybean acreage, it could support market prices (depending on the foreign production response) and limit LDP's for soybeans, although payments for these other crops could increase. The setting of loan rate minimums can be viewed as arbitrary and incapable of signaling a new response to short-term market conditions. So, adjusting loan rate minimums may only alter which commodities are in greatest disequilibrium.

Production Flexibility Contract (PFC) Payments

Payments under Production Flexibility Contracts (PFCs) are based on historical base acres and yields, and are thus completely decoupled from current production decisions. Likewise, market loss assistance payments (MLA) under the emergency ad hoc assistance bills have been tied to historical base acreage and payment yield. As such, neither of these payments necessarily goes to current crop producers, but to those who own farms with base acreage. Since oilseeds were not a part of the former system of crop base acres, none of the fixed PFC or MLA payments that farmers now receive are based on past oilseed acreage.

To compensate oilseed farmers experiencing poor market conditions, the government authorised $475 million in oilseed assistance in 1999 and $500 million for 2000 crops. Some proposals would formally include oilseeds into the PFC payments by adding $0.5-$1.7 billion to current annual expenditures of $4 billion. These new PFC payments would be based on a farmer's oilseeds acreage and yield for a previous time period.

Countercyclical Income Support

Some have criticised the fixed PFC payments as being an inadequate response during times of greatest need.

Instead of passing annual emergency economic assistance bills, supporters recommend a new programme to offset crop revenue shortfalls due to poor yields or low prices. Generally, the plans would initiate countercyclical payments whenever some measure of national or regional programme crop income per acre fails to meet a minimum percentage for a fixedbase reference period. There are several approaches for the countercyclical payments that differ on the specifics of the trigger mechanism. In contrast, some groups call for a complete return to mandatory or voluntary supply management policies, such as acreage idling and grain reserves, to support commodity prices above total costs of production.

But numerous studies have documented how supply restrictions discourage exports, raise production costs, and disrupt local agricultural economies. Previous studies with the farmer-owned reserve has identified the difficulty of raising prices over the long term through stock management. Supply controls also overlook the response of foreign producers to expand output when U.S. prices rise, requiring ever tighter restrictions (or even import barriers) to maintain farm price levels.

Brazil alone has undeveloped farmland potential that exceeds the acreage that the United States currently plants to both soybeans and corn. That acreage could easily be brought into production with higher prices. The high Federal costs of storage subsidies would only be exacerbated as uncompetitively priced U.S. crops lose export market share.

Conservation Payments

The incomes of many farmers are supplemented by environmental payment and costshare programmes including the Conservation Reserve Programme, the Wetlands Reserve Programme, and the Environmental Quality Incentives Programme. The services that farmers render include reducing soil erosion and groundwater pollution, restoring natural wetlands from farming, and improving wildlife habitat. Some critics have charged that the primary objective behind previous conservation programmes was to support farm prices and incomes by taking land out of production, while a comprehensive and cost-effective delivery of environmental benefits was secondary. In response, under most proposals, conservation programme payments would be continued but with better targeting to all farmers that achieve real environmental benefits and a broader scope of goals, such as green space preservation and carbon sequestration (to resist global warming from greenhouse gases).

Other Issues

All agricultural programmes support farmland values. Despite low market prices, government payments have sustained cash flow, and the balance sheets of many farmland owners have remained relatively strong. Thus, the value of farm assets can affect borrowing, leasing, and transfer decisions. Farms with large equity are better able to withstand periods of low prices than farms with high debt or more modest net assets. Higher land values also lead to higher cash rents for tenant farmers, raising their costs of production.

Many young farmers get their start by inheriting property, so estate taxes can be another hurdle in preserving some large family farms. Some question the fairness of having the largest and most efficient farmowners reap the bulk of government subsidies while smaller, full-time farm operators receive too little support to remain financially viable, so targeting of payments may be a focus of debate. Conversely, some farm groups would eliminate all payment limitations on farm programmes because of their ineffectiveness and high administrative costs.

Biodiesel has been promoted as a way to improve air quality, and advocates contend that including it in a renewable fuels programme would support domestic consumption of vegetable oils and farm prices for oilseeds. In a new bioenergy programme, USDA will make $300 million available to eligible bioenergy producers in fiscal 2001 and 2002 to offset a portion of their commodity purchases needed to expand production and capacity. Similarly, research that supports development of environmentally friendly agricultural-based materials (such as biodegradable lubricants, adhesives, plastics, and inks) may result in new, commercially significant product markets for oilseed producers.

WTO Compatibility

In the last decade, U.S. bilateral and multilateral trade agreements such as NAFTA and the Uruguay Round Agreement on Agriculture (URAA) have widened access to foreign oilseed and oilseed product markets. Under the URAA, countries agreed to reduce the volume and value of export subsidies, lower average import tariffs, and eliminate import quotas. Yet, maintaining commitments for minimising distortions to international trade also constrains the design of domestic agricultural supports. Policies linked to current production (such as price supports, input subsidies, and marketing loan benefits) can induce overproduction of crops, which affects imports and exports.

The United States and other developed nations also agreed to limit, by the year 2000, the aggregate value of trade-distorting domestic farm supports (the so-called amber box) to 80 percent of a 1986-88 base ($19.1 billion in 2000). An extension of NAFTA to the rest of the Western Hemisphere or a new WTO round of trade negotiations will likely involve further reductions in export subsidies, tariffs, and domestic agricultural supports.

Government programmes that are decoupled from current agricultural prices, production, and resource use do not count toward the maximum allowable limit on tradedistorting support. These "green box" programmes have the smallest effect on production and trade and for the United States include domestic food aid, conservation payments, natural disaster relief, and PFC income supports. If based on historic rather than current prices and production, a countercyclical income support programme, its advocates believe, would also meet these criteria.

The United States has notified the WTO that crop market loss assistance payments (MLA) mandated by recent emergency legislation are non-product-specific amber box payments. As with the green box PFC, each producer's share of the total amount of MLA available in a given year is determined by past programme participation and not by current production or resource use. MLA payments are distributed, in fact, in proportion to PFC payments. However, the PFC totals were predetermined by the 1996 Farm Act while the MLA payments were legislated annually in response to recent market price experiences. Consequently, the MLA payments may be assumed to be related to market prices after the PFC (or WTO) base period, making the MLA ineligible for the green box.

9

Technological Measures to Prevent Seed and Plant Varieties

The Rural Advancement Foundation International (RAFI) is an international civil society organisation, headquartered in Canada, with an affiliate office in Pittsboro, North Carolina (USA). RAFI is concerned about the loss of biological diversity-especially in agriculture - and about the impact of intellectual property on farmers and world food security.

Challenges to Agricultural Biodiversity

There are three trends that are the major challenges facing conservation and sustainable use of agricultural biodiversity. The first trend, and probably the most obvious one, is genetic erosion. We're losing genetic resources for agriculture at an unprecedented rate. What's at stake is the biological basis for world food security. Forests are falling, fisheries are collapsing, plant and animal genetic diversity is eroding all over the world. The statistics are sobering:

— Crop genetic resources are disappearing at the rate of 1-2% per annum.

- — Domestic animal breeds are disappearing at an annual rate of 5%, or 6 breeds per month. FAO considers 30% of all livestock breeds endangered or critical.
- — Tropical forests are falling at a rate of just under 1% per annum, or 29 hectares per minute (CGIAR 1996). From 1980-1990, this is equivalent to an area the size of Ecuador and Peru combined.
- — All of the world's main fishing grounds are being fished at or beyond their limits. About 70% of the world's conventional marine species are fully exploited, over-exploited, depleted or in the process of recovering from over fishing. During this century, about 980 fish species have become threatened.

The loss of biodiversity threatens global food security, especially for the poor, who rely on biodiversity for 85 to 90% of their livelihood needs.

The second trend is privatisation of plant breeding and seed sales. The first half of 1998 witnessed a dramatic consolidation of power over plant genetic resources worldwide, a trend that began over three decades ago. The global seed trade is now dominated by "life industry" corporations whose vast economic power has effectively marginalised the role of public sector plant breeding and research. Of course, the consolidation trend is not just in seeds but in all sectors of the life industry.

- — 20 years ago there were thousands of seed companies, most of which were small and family owned. Today, the top 10 global seed companies control 30% of the $23 billion commercial seed trade.

— 20 years ago RAFI was monitoring about 65 agrochemical companies involved in the development of new crop chemicals. Today the top 10 pesticide manufacturers account for 82% of the $30 billion dollar global market.

— Two decades ago, the top 20 global pharmaceutical companies controlled roughly 5% of the global pharmaceutical trade. Today, the top 10 pharmaceutical companies account for 36% of the $251 billion global pharmaceutical market.

— Today, the top 10 firms held 61% of the animal veterinary market valued at (US) $16 billion. If you look at the dominant companies in all of these sectors-in plant breeding, pesticides, veterinary medicines, and pharmaceuticals-you'll find that many of the same companies are dominant in all of these sectors. Companies such as Monsanto, Novartis, Dow, and Dupont are everywhere.

The bottom line is that fewer and fewer companies are making critical decisions about the agricultural research agenda, and the future of agriculture worldwide. With the advent of genetic engineering life industry corporations are staking far-reaching claims of ownership over a vast array of living organisms and biological processes. The power of exclusive monopoly patents is giving these companies the legal right to determine who gets access to proprietary science and at what price. This has serious implications for the future of world food security and for conservation of genetic resources.

The third trend, mention has to do with farmers and their role in conserving and using agricultural biodiversity. The future of world food security depends not just on stored crop genes, but on the people who use and maintain crop genetic diversity on a daily basis. In the long run, the conservation of plant genetic diversity depends not so much on a small number of institutional plant breeders, but on the vast number of farmers who select, improve, and use crop diversity, especially in marginal farming environments.

That's why we are particularly alarmed by the current trend to eliminate the right of farmers to save and exchange seed, and breed their own crops. Both public and private sector institutions are using, developing, and promoting a variety of legal and technological tools that are designed to give the seed industry greater control over plant genetics and eliminate the right of farmers to save and re-plant seed from their harvest.

Farmers are not just saving seeds, they are plant breeders who are constantly adapting their crops to specific farming conditions and needs. For over 200 generations, farmers have been selecting seeds and adapting their plants for local use. This genetic diversity is key to maintaining and improving the world's food supply. No plant breeder or genetic engineer starts from scratch when they develop a new cultivar of maize, or tomato, or barley. They are building on the accumulated success of generations of farmers, who have selected and improved seeds for thousands of years. Companies like Dupont and Monsanto and Novartis tell us that they 'invented' their genetically engineered plants and that they should be rewarded with exclusive monopoly patents. In reality, corporate plant breeders are fine-tuning and modifying plants that were developed by anonymous farmers and the more recent contributions of institutional plant breeders.

Intellectual property regimes have evolved very rapidly. Eighteen years ago, RAFI testified at Congressional hearings in Washington, DC on US plant variety protection laws-a type of plant patenting. Gary Nabhan also testified at those hearings.

Under US patent law, it's now illegal for farmers to save patented seed and re-use it. Today, Monsanto requires farmer's-its customers -to sign a gene licensing agreement before they buy the company's patented, genetically engineered seeds. If farmers are caught infringing the patent, Monsanto is "vigorously prosecuting" them in court. The penalties may include criminal charges, on-farm field inspections, and damages that could exceed $1 million dollars. In some areas, the company has hired Pinkerton investigators to root-out farmers who are saving Monsanto's patented seed. In other words, farmers are being turned into criminals and rural communities are becoming corporate police states. Monsanto has spent over $8 billion acquiring seed and biotech companies since 1996, and it's now the second largest seed corporation in the world.

Historically, plant variety protection regimes guaranteed the right of farmers to save seed from their harvest. But the farmers' right or farmers' exemption is disappearing from international plant patenting regimes. Earlier this year, the 1991 Act of UPOV entered into force, replacing the 1978 Act. UPOV is the international body that coordinates a common legal regime for plant variety protection. Under the new Act, the farmers' right to save seed is no longer an automatic feature of the new Convention-it is recognised only if member states make special provision for it in national legislation. This is a big deal because many nations of the South are under intense pressure to join UPOV to satisfy their obligation under GATT-TRIPs.

Terminator Technology

The latest assault on the right of farmers to save seed is a technology developed by USDA and the seed industry. In March of this year the USDA and Delta & Pine Land Co., a Monsanto subsidiary, proudly announced that they received a patent on a technique that genetically alters seed so that it will not germinate if re-planted the following season. In other words, scientists have developed plants that are genetically engineered to kill their own seeds. The technology is designed to prevent farmers from saving seed from their harvest, thus forcing them to return to the commercial seed market every year. This technology is still in the early stages of development. But, if it works as advertised, it's a dream-come-true for the multinational seed industry. Because its view as a potentially "lethal" technology, RAFI calls it the "Terminator Technology."

Probably some of you know that RAFI and many other NGOs have adopted a campaign to ban the Terminator. In RAFI's opinion, the Terminator technology is the neutron bomb of agriculture. It's a dead-end for farmers, and for biological diversity. This is a product that will bring no agronomic benefit to farmers or consumers-it's designed simply to increase seed industry profits. The technology is aimed primarily at seed markets in Africa, Asia, and Latin America, where over 1.4 billion people depend on farm-saved seed and onfarm plant breeding. Patents on the Terminator technology are pending in 87 foreign countries. The president of Delta & Pine Land, Murray Robinson, says that his company's seed sterilising technology could be used on up to 1 billion acres (400 million ha) worldwide (an area the size of South Asia), and that it could generate revenues for his company in excess of $1 billion per annum.

If farmers lose the right to save seed-they lose the ability to select seed and adapt crops to their unique farming conditions. If farmers eat or abandon their traditional seeds in the process of adopting this new technology, centuries of crop genetic diversity will be lost forever. But that's not all. Scientists warn that, under certain conditions, the trait for seed sterility will flow, via pollen, from Terminator crops to surrounding plants, making the seeds of neighbouring plants sterile. Simply put, the Terminator technology will restrict the food-producing capacity of farmers and it will destroy diversity.

The highly unpopular Terminator technology has catalysed international debate on these issues and there's an avalanche of public opposition. Over 2,500 people have written to US Secretary of Agriculture Glickman urging him to cease negotiations with Monsanto on the licensing of the technology, and to abandon development of the technology. Two weeks ago, the world's largest international agricultural research network-the Consultative Group on International Agricultural Research -adopted a policy banning the use of Terminator technology (and other genetic seed sterilisation technologies) in its plant breeding programs.

— African delegates to the United Nations FAO have said that they don't want Terminator genes used on African soil.

— In May, the Conference of the Parties to the Convention on Biological Diversity (COP IV) directed its scientific body to examine the technology's impact on farmers and biodiversity.

— India's agriculture minister has taken action to ban the import of seeds containing the terminator gene because of the potential harm to Indian agriculture.

If the US government is serious about supporting the conservation and sustainable use of biodiversity, then it's sending precisely the wrong message by developing a technology that aims to restrict the right of farmers to save seed and select crops. The right to save seed is fundamental to agriculture and global food security.

10

Seed Legislation in India

In 2004 two laws have been proposed – a seed Act and a Patent Ordinance which could forever destroy the biodiversity of Indian seeds and crops, and rob farmers of all freedoms, establishing a seed dictatorship. Eighty per cent of all seed in India is still saved by farmers. Farmers indigenous varieties are the basis of our ecological and food security. Coastal farmers have evolved salt resistant varieties.

Bihar and Bengal farmers have evolved flood resistant varieties, farmers of Rajasthan and the semi-arid Deccan have evolved drought resistant varieties, Himalayan farmers have evolved frost resistant varieties. Pulses, millets, oilseeds, rices, wheats, vegetables provide the diverse basis of our health and nutrition security. This is the sector being targeted by the Seed Act. These seeds are indigenous farmers varieties of diverse crops – thousands of rices, hundreds of wheats, oilseeds such as linseed, sesame, groundnut, coconut, pulses including gahat, narrangi, rajma, urad, moong, masur, tur, vegetables and fruits.

The Seed Act is designed to "enclose" the free economy of farmers seed varieties. Once farmers seed supply is destroyed through compulsory registration by making it illegal to plant unlicensed varieties, farmers are pushed into dependency on corporate monopoly of patented seed. The Seed Act is therefore the handmaiden of the Patent Amendment Acts which have introduced patents on seed.

New IPR laws are creating monopolies over seeds and plant genetic resources. Seed saving and seed exchange, basic freedoms of farmers, are being redefined. There are many examples of how Seed Acts in various countries and the introduction of IPRs prevent farmers from engaging in their own seed production. Josef Albrecht, an organic farmer in Germany, was not satisfied with the commercially available seed. He worked and developed his own ecological varieties of wheat. Ten other organic farmers from neighbouring villages took his wheat seeds. Albrecht was fined by his government because he traded in uncertified seed. He has challenged the penalty and the Seed Act because he feels restricted in freely exercising his occupation as an organic farmer by this law.

In Scotland, there are a large number of farmers who grow seed potato and sell seed potato to other farmers. They could, until the early 1990s, freely sell the reproductive material to other seed potato growers, to merchants, or to farmers. In the 1990s, holders of plant breeders' rights started to issue notices to potato growers through the British Society of Plant Breeders and made selling of seed potato by farmers to other farmers illegal. Seed potato growers had to grow varieties under contract to the seed industry, which specified the price at which the contracting company would take back the crop and barred growers from selling the crop to anyone.

Soon, the companies started to reduce the acreage and prices. In 1994, seed potato bought from Scottish farmers for £140 was sold for more than double that price to English farmers, whilst the two sets of farmers were prevented from dealing directly with each other. Seed potato growers signed a petition complaining about the stranglehold of a few companies acting as a 'cartel'. They also started to sell non-certified seed directly to English farmers. The seed industry claimed they were losing £4 million in seed sales through the direct sale of uncertified seed potato between farmers.

In February 1995, the British Society for Plant Breeders decided to proceed with a high profile court case against a farmer from Aberdeenshire. The farmer was forced to pay £30,000 as compensation to cover royalties lost to the seed industry by direct farmer-to-farmer exchange. Existing United Kingdom and European Union laws thus prevent farmers from exchanging uncertified seed as well as protected varieties.

In the US as well, farmer-to-farmer exchange has been made illegal. Dennis and Becky Winterboer were farmers owning a 500-acre farm in Iowa. Since 1987, the Winterboers have derived a sizeable portion of their income from 'brown bagging' sales of their crops to other farmers to use as seed. A 'brown bag' sale occurs when a farmer plants seeds in his own field and then sells the harvest as seed to other farmers. Asgrow (a commercial company which has plant variety protection for its soybean seeds) filed suit against the Winterboers on the grounds that its property rights were being violated. The Winterboers argued that they had acted within the law since according to the Plant Variety Act farmers had the right to sell seed, provided both the farmer and seller were farmers. Subsequently, in 1994, the Plant Variety Act was amended, and the farmers' privilege to save and exchange seed was amended, establishing absolute monopoly of the seed industry by making farmer-to-farmer exchange and sales illegal.

Similar laws are being introduced in India. The entire country is being taken for a ride with the introduction of the Seed Act 2004 on grounds that the Act is needed to guarantee seed quality. However, the Seed Act 1966 already performs the function of seed testing and seed certification. Twenty labs have been declared as seed testing labs under the 1966 Act in different States. Nine seed corporations have been identified as certification agencies. Under pressure from World Bank the Seed Policy of 1988 started to dismantle our robust public sector seed supply system, which accounted for 20% of the seeds farmers grow. Eighty per cent of the seed prior to globalisation is the farmers' own varieties, which have been saved, exchanged and reproduced freely and have guaranteed our food security.

The introduction of 2004 Seed Act needs to be assessed in the context of the simultaneous introduction of the 3rd Patent (Amendment) Act. Our 1970 Patent Law has been changed under the coercive pressure of WTO in spite of the overdue mandatory TRIPS review. Patents will now been granted for seeds, plants, micro-organisms, cells and even GMO's and animals. Quite clearly a monopolistic patent regime cannot be established as long as farmers have the alternative of their own zero cost, reliable, time tested high value seeds of their traditional varieties of indigenous agro-biodiversity.

The Seed Act 2004 has one and only one objective of stopping farmers from seed saving, seed exchange and seed reproduction. In the objective the 2004 Act clearly states that it is aimed at replacing farmers saved seeds with seeds from private seed industries. The repeated reference to 'barter' in the Seed Act will prevent farmer's exchange, a necessary aspect of maintaining high quality seed supply at the community level.

Further the compulsory registration of seed combined with the power of seed inspectors to enter and search premises, the power to break open any container and any door is tantamount to creating a 'Seed Police' to terrorise farmers who are conserving biodiversity and practicing a sovereign self-reliant agriculture. The fine for seed exchange and barter of unregistered seed. While criminalising farmers who consume biodiversity and traditional varieties, the Seed Act fails to do one thing it should have done, which is to regulate and hold liable private seed industry for seed failure and genetic contamination from GMO's. For Example the failure of maize seeds in Bihar last year cost more than 1000 crores to Bihar farmers and the constant failure of Bt. cotton annually is costing more than a billion dollars to Indian farmers.

In the new Seed Act farmers can only claim compensation under the Consumer Protection Act. This option is in any way is available to the farmers presently and the brutal power of the Central Authority, which acts to prevent farmers from growing own seeds, provides no safety and remedy to our farmers from untested and hazardous seeds MNCs are selling in the Indian market.

The Seed Act has also undermined the role of the State governments. The Central Seed Committee in 1966 Act has representatives nominated by the government of each State. Now only 5 State will be represented in the Central Seed Committee and even these will be nominated not by the State governments but by the Centre.

The 2004 Seed Act has nothing positive to offer to farmers of India but offer a promise of a monopoly to private seed industries, which has already pushed thousands of our farmers to suicide through dependency and debt caused by unreliable, high dependency and non-renewable seeds.

The 1966 Act has served the country well and should continue to provide the framework for seed testing and seed certification. Farmer varieties and indigenous agro-biodiversity is already been registered by Local Biodiversity Committee through Community Biodiversity Registers (CBRs). We do not need a Centralised Seed Authority with police power which uses compulsory registration to prevent farmers from growing, saving and exchanging their own seeds. It is the MNC seed industry that need regulation and not the small farmers of our country without whose seed freedom the country will have no food sovereignty and food security.

Product Patent

Methods of agriculture and plants were excluded from patentability in the Indian Patent Act 1970 to ensure that the seed, the first link in the food chain, was held as a common property resource in the public domain. In this manner, it guaranteed farmers the inalienable right to save, exchange and improve upon the seed was not violated.

But recently, two amendments have been made in the 1970 Patent Act. The 2nd Amendment makes changes in the definition of what is NOT an invention. This has opened the flood gates for the patenting of genetically engineered seeds.

According to Section 3(j) of the Indian Patent Act, the following is not an invention:

> Any process for the medical, surgical, creative, prophylactic or other treatment of human beings or any

> process for a similar treatment of animals or plants or render them free of disease or to increase their economic value or that of their products.

In the 2nd Amendment however, the mention of "plants" have been deleted from this section. This deletion implies that a method or process modification of a plant can now be counted as an invention and therefore can be patented. Thus the method of producing Bt. cotton by introducing genes of a bacterium thurengerisis in cotton to produce toxins to kill the bollworm can now be covered by the exclusive rights associated with patents. In other words, Monsanto can now have Bt. cotton patents in India.

The Second Amendment has also added a new section (3j). This section allows for the production or propagation of genetically engineered plants to count as an invention. Its status as an invention thus deems it. But this section excludes as inventions "plants and animals including seeds, varieties and species and essentially biological processes for production or propagation of plants and animals". Since plants produced through the use of new biotechnologies are not technically considered "essentially biological," section 3j has found another way to create room for Monsanto. This loophole, couched in the guise of scientific advancement, thus allows patents on GMOs and hence opens the flood gate for patenting transgenic plants.

What is most concerning is how the language of section 3j is a verbatim translation into India law of Article 27.3 (b) of TRIPS Agreement. Article 27.3 (b) of TRIPS states:

> Parties may exclude from patentability plants and animals other than micro-organisms, and essentially biological processes for the production of plants or animals other than non-biological and microbiological processes. However, parties shall provide for the

> protection of plant varieties either by patents or by an effective sui generis system or by any combination thereof. This provision shall be reviewed four years after the entry into force of the Agreement establishing the W.T.O.

As Monsanto had a hand in drafting the TRIPS agreement, it is not surprising that the Monsanto Amendments have also made their way into India's patent laws.

However, Article 27.3(b) is under review. The Government should have insisted on the completion of the review, a commitment of the Doha Round, instead of changing India's Patent Law. As a result of sustained public pressure, after the agreement came into force in 1995, many Third World countries made recommendations for changes in Article 27.3 (b) to prevent biopiracy. India, in its discussion paper submitted to the TRIPS Council stated:

"Patenting of life forms may have at least two dimensions. Firstly, there is the ethical question of the extent of private ownership that could be extended to life forms. The second dimension relates to the use of IPRs' concept as understood in the industrialised world and its appropriateness in the face of the larger dimension of rights on knowledge, their ownership, use, transfer and dissemination

Informal system, e.g. the shrutis and in the Indian tradition and grandmother's portions all over the world get scant recognition. To create systems that fail to address this issue can have severe adverse consequences on mankind, some say even leading to extinction.

Patents on seeds are a necessary aspect of the corporate deployment of GM seeds and crops. When combined with the ecological risks of genetically engineered seeds like Bt. cotton, seed patents create a context of total control over the seed sector, and hence over our food and agricultural security. Looking with closer analysis, there are three ways that the 2nd Amendment and 3rd Amendment of the Indian Patent laws have jeopardised our seed and food security, and hence our national security.

Firstly, it allows patents on seeds and plants through sections 3(i) and 3(j), as we saw above. Patents are monopolies and exclusive rights which prevent farmers from saving seeds; and seed companies from producing seeds. Patents on seeds transform seed saving into an "intellectual property crime".

Secondly, genetic pollution is inevitable. Monsanto will use the patents and pollution to claim ownership of crops on farmers' fields where the Bt. gene has reached it through wind or pollinators. This has been established as precedence in the case of a Canadian farmer, Percy Schmeiser, whose canola field was contaminated by Monsanto's "Round up Ready Canola," but instead of Monsanto paying Percy on the basis of the pollute principle, Monsanto demanded $200,000 fine for "theft" of Monsanto's "intellectual property". Thousands of U.S. farmers also have been sued. Will Indian farmers be blamed for theft when Monsanto's GM cotton contaminates their crops? Or will the government wake up and enforce strict monitoring and liability?

When combined with the 3rd product patents amendment, these changes can mean absolute monopoly. A decision on a plant patent infringement suit has set a new precedent for interpreting plant patent coverage. In countries, where plant patents are not allowed, patenting genes is available as an opening for patenting properties and characteristics of the plant, and hence having exclusive rights to those properties and characteristics.

Patent protection implies the exclusion of farmers' right over the resources having these genes and characteristics. This will undermine the very foundations of agriculture. For example, a patent has been granted in the U.S. to a biotechnology company, Sungene, for a sunflower variety with very high oleic acid content. The claim was for the characteristic (i.e., high oleic acid) and not just for the genes producing the characteristic. Sungene has notified others involved in sunflower breeding that the development of any variety high in oleic acid will be considered an infringement of its patent.

Corporate Rights and Farmers Rights

New Intellectual Property Rights (IPR) legislation is being introduced in the area of plant genetic resources (PGR) under pressure of the U.S. government as well as the requirements of the TRIPS agreement of the W.T.O. while W.T.O. gives a five year transition period to introduce PGR legislation, the U.S. pressure was to introduce such legislation immediately. Further, the U.S. has been demanding monopoly protection for Transnational Corporations (TNCs) which control the seed industry. On the other hand people's organisations are fighting to protect farmers' rights to their biodiversity and their right to survival as well as the freedom of scientists to work for the removal of hunger rather than corporate profits.

Farmers organisations, biodiversity conservation groups, sustainable agriculture networks and public interest oriented scientists are trying to ensure that farmers' rights are protected, and through the protection of farmers' rights, sovereign control over our biological wealth and its sustainable use in agricultural production is ensured. The conflict over PGR legislation is a conflict between farmers and the seed industry and between the public domain and private profits, between an agriculture that produces and reproduces diversity and one that consumes diversity and produces uniformity.

On January 29, 1996 at an address at the Indian Institute of Agricultural Research, the Unite States Secretary of Agriculture, Mr. Daniel Glickman directly addressed the issue of the protection of seed Multinationals (MNCs). He said, "I hope our new legislation will provide a responsible and reasonable protection to private seed companies, which will encourage them to provide the best seeds available for your farmers. There would be very few inventions of anything, particularly in agriculture, without patent protection because it is the fundamental fact of nature that people will not go through the expense of development of new ideas just for the altruistic benefit of the human race.

In other words, what the U.S. government is coercing the Indian government to do is introduce unhealthy fat and meat rich diets through the expansion of U.S. agribusiness, agroprocessing and fast food industry. The proposal is to replace the small peasant and farmer based agricultural economy of India with agribusiness controlled industrial agriculture. This shift is associated with a transformation of farmers as breeders and reproducers of their own seed supply to farmers as consumers of propriety seed from the seed industry. It is also a shift from a food economy based on million of farmers as autonomous producers to a food system controlled by a handful of TNCs which control both inputs and outputs. This is a recipe for food insecurity, biodiversity erosion and uprooting of farmers from the land.

It is often stated that IPRs will not stop traditional farmers from using native seeds. However, the Seed Act 2004 is designed to do just that. Further when it is recognised that IPRs are an essential part of a package of agribusiness controlled agriculture in which farmers no longer grow native seeds but seeds supplied by the TNC seed industry, IPRs become a means of monopoly that wipe out farmers rights to save and exchange seed.

This leads to TNC totalitarianism in agriculture. TNCs will decide what is grown by farmers, what they use as inputs, and when they sell their produce, to whom and at what price. they will also decide what is eaten by consumers, at what price, with what content and how much information is made available to them about the nature of food commodities.

IPRs are a significant instrument for the establishment of this TNC totalitarianism. The protection of the rights of citizens as producers and consumers needs the forging of new concepts and categories, new instruments and mechanism to counter and limit the monopoly power of TNCs in agriculture. Community rights are an important balancing concept for protecting the public interest in the context of IPR protection for corporations.

In the field of food and agriculture, farmers' rights are the countervailing force to breeders rights and patents on seed and plant material. Farmers' rights in the context of monopoly control of the food system become relevant not just for farming communities, but also consumers. They are necessary not just for the survival of the people but also for the survival of the country. Without sovereign rights of farming communities to their seed an plant genetic resources, there can be no sovereignty of the country.

Farmers' rights are an ecological, economic, cultural and political imperative. Without community rights, agricultural communities cannot protect agricultural biodiversity. This biodiversity is necessary not just for the ecological insurance of agriculture. Rights to agricultural biodiversity is also an economic imperative because without it our farmers and our country will loose their freedom and options for survival. Since biodiversity and cultural diversity are intimately linked, conservation of agricultural biodiversity is a cultural imperative also. Finally, without farmers' rights, there is no political mechanism to limit monopolies in agriculture and inevitable consequence of displacement, hunger and famine that will follow total monopoly control over food production and consumption through the monopoly ownership over seed, the first link in the food chain.

India's new Seed Bill

In 2004, a new Seed Bill was announced. So why the need for change? Proponents of the new Seeds Bill list a number of supposed deficiencies in the 1996 Seeds Act to be fixed, including:

- To make the registration of varieties obligatory (previously voluntary)
- Creation of a comprehensive National Register of Seeds
- To regulate (make easier) the imports and exports of seeds
- New regulations on GM crops
- To improve market conditions for private seed companies

Mandatory Registration and the National Register of Seeds

The proposed new seed law introduces the concept of

mandatory registration of all seeds for sale. In other words, all marketed seed and planting material, whether domestic or foreign, will have to be registered. This is a significant change from the existing law, which sought to regulate the quality of only a limited number of varieties notified under the law. Now, however, any seed for sowing or planting cannot be sold unless it is registered.

All registered varieties will be recorded in a National Register of Seeds database. Registration will be granted for new varieties for a period of 15 years in the case of annual & biennial crops and 18 years for long duration perennials. As with registered varieties in other parts of the world, varieties need to be field-tested to determine their VCU (Value for Cultivation and Use). In addition, seeds need to be correctly labelled on their containers, including genetically modified seeds. Furthermore, seed producers, seed processing units, seed dealers and horticulture nurseries all have to be registered with the government of the State in which they operate.

GM Seeds

The regulatory system governing GM crops is in the process of being revamped with the National Biotechnology Development Strategy. It is clear from the draft strategy that the government will be supporting the further introduction of GM crops. The new Seeds Bill follows this same line and does not prohibit the registration of GM seeds. Registration of transgenic seeds is however subject to environmental clearance under the Environment Protection law. However, in a gesture to keep critics quiet, the Seeds Bill does ban the use of Terminator seeds.

Exporting and Importing Seeds

Under the new Seed Bill all imported seeds will also need

to be registered, though the government may allow the import of an unregistered seed for research purposes. Apart from the registration of imported seeds, the new Bill does not make any other provisions, such as for phytosanitary standards, which still rely on other existing legislation. However, the main basis for the registration of imported seeds is to support larger companies importing seed, which has been increasing substantially recently. For example in 2001 to 2002, imports were around 860 tonnes, but within one year, this had increased to 1,766 tonnes, with a value of US$ 18 million, 20% of which comes from the US. Exports of seed are even more valuable at around US$ 21 million for the same year (2002-2003).

Benefit of the Farmer

The official government line, when arguing in favour of this bill, is that *"if we don't know who is selling the seeds, we cannot control their quality"*. This, of course, is the same argument used by the seed industry around the world. So this new law is being presented as a "consumer protection" act for farmers. In the light of several reports of farmers' suicides and crop failure this has found favour with many unsuspecting civil society groups. So will this law be good news for farmers? What protection do farmers get if their legally-bought registered-varieties fail? Interestingly, farmers at this point can only turn to the Consumer Protection Act of 1986, an option which is available today without any new legislation. Meanwhile, the Indian Seed Industry is lobbying for the removal of seeds from the Consumer Protection Act.

T. Ramanaiah, a cotton farmer from Andhra Pradesh, is currently fighting a case to get compensation for very poor yields in the District Consumer Court, an option which is by its very nature a tedious one without any guarantee of success. His struggle has inspired activists to put together a legal manual for farmers seeking compensation for failed yields. Often, even if a government recognises that farmers' need to be compensated, the company might not be ready to pay up.

In the State of Andhra Pradesh when farmers suffered losses from cultivating Monsanto's Bt cotton, Monsanto was only willing to pay for failure to germinate and for absence of the genetic purity promised by the company, and not for yield losses. The Plant Variety Protection (PVP) law of India does make provision for farmers to claim, via a PVP Authority, compensation from the breeder of a variety if it does not perform as expected, though such a body has not yet been set up. Such a body, when formed, would only rule on varieties which are PVP registered and such decisions would be on a discretionary basis.

The bill is essentially about seed registration and certification, but in mandating that only registered seed will be sold, it is not only about what it regulates but about what it does not. By mandating what the market will offer, it determines what it excludes. So what is in the Bill for the small farmer? Once again the proponents of the Seed Bill come rushing with their answer: *"Exemption for farmers to save, use, exchange, share or sell their seed without registration"*. Indeed the law does state that: "[nothing] *shall restrict the right of the farmer to save, use, exchange, share or sell his farm seeds and planting material"*

However, it continues with: *"except that he shall not sell such seed or planting material under a brand name or which does not conform to the minimum limit of germination, physical purity, genetic purity prescribed..."*

So there is the catch—farmers cannot sell their seeds if they do not meet the standards of registration. Nor can farmers use a brand name and enter the seed trade. For the seed industry this is music to their ears; with this small piece of legislation all competition from non-registered seeds is done away with. Although farmer-to-farmer seed exchange can continue despite the proposed law, the ambiguity in the exception clause, coupled with wide powers given to Seed Inspectors, makes farmers anxious about how their small local sales, for instance in the village fairs, would be regulated. Even though today farmers produce around 80% of India's seed, selling their own seed is now being restricted. In reality, only formal breeders and big businesses can get their seeds registered.

So why don't farmers simply get their seeds registered? In this way, they could legally sell their home-grown varieties of seeds. However, under the proposed system it makes it impossible for farmers to register varieties. The process takes a long time, is extremely expensive for a farmer, and anyway farmers' seeds would probably fail to pass the required standards. A farmers' breeding criteria are very broad, incorporating ecological and social factors, rather than only yield; what is exchanged between farmers is determined by local needs and therefore farmers' varieties are best regulated by farmers themselves. As a result, there are some in India advocating for a community certification process by, and for, small-scale farmers.

Farmers can, therefore, sell harvested seed which is a registered variety. But the problem here is that if the registered seed is also PVP-protected then the farmer is again prohibited by the PVP legislation from selling branded seed in the market. As for farmers' varieties of crops, the very crops that they have been growing, exchanging and selling for many generations, evidence from around the world shows that these will die out. By following the letter of the law, there will be little incentive to grow and use farmer varieties and farmers will have no choice but to buy and use registered seed from a private company. On the other hand, many farmers are likely to ignore the law on the sale of seeds and indeed stopping the sale of farmers' seeds will be very difficult to enforce. Indeed, the very survival of farmers' varieties may be very dependent on farmers simply ignoring this aspect of the law and continuing to sell and buy their own farmer varieties.

The Bill has come under severe criticism countrywide from all sectors of society, including farmers' groups and numerous non-governmental organisations. The demands range from a complete withdrawal of the proposed Seed Bill 2004 to the recognition of farmers' absolute rights to indigenous seeds. Widespread campaigns and mass actions continue to be planned at the village and district levels. Farmers are directing their ire at what they regard as restrictions on their time-honoured freedom to grow and sow as they please. They also see the Bill as an erosion of their rights to sell seeds and are dissatisfied with the lack of provision for corporate liability, be it for Indian or foreign seed companies.

Other problems cited with the Bill include:

1. *Consolidation of the private sector*: Many fear that the Bill will hand over the seed business to seed transnational corporations.
2. *Introduction of GMOs*: There is growing concern that the Bill will ease entry of GM crops with the possible contamination of traditional varieties with GM agriculture.
3. *Prices*: Many believe that seed prices will go up. Private companies would need to recover the costs

of registration which would be passed onto farmers.

4. *Centralising power*: Many are concerned that the Seed Bill will move decision-making away from the state level. Under the Indian constitution, agriculture is under the jurisdiction of the state, with the exception of cotton and oil seeds, and tradable commodities. The central government treats seeds as a "tradable commodity" to constitutionally justify its lawmaking on the subject.

Seed Bill for the Private Sector

The main beneficiaries of this new law are clearly the private seed sector. With the opening up of the seed market only to those who are able to certify and register seeds, coupled with the suppression of the sale of farmer's varieties, it is in particular the transnational corporations that will benefit. Such corporations make up an estimated 30% share of the market. However, large Indian companies will also benefit through sales of exported seed. With an extensive and rich agricultural genetic resource base, coupled with the associated knowledge and cheap labour provides a fertile ground for seed production.

Asia is becoming the largest seed market in the world and is the biggest agricultural trading partner for the US. The US Department of Commerce has identified India as one of the world's top ten *"Big Emerging Markets"*. With China the largest seed producer, India is in second place. The US government is taking special interest in the economic and legislative "reforms" in this part of the world, as in India it is keen to encourage conformity to US standards and to simplify seed trade.

Seed legislations were originally meant to be about government being able to ensure good quality seed and safeguard farmers from bad seed distributed by industry. The trend however seems to show, among other things, how industry standards are being adopted by the seed laws, which themselves are becoming a means to facilitate the entry of transnational corporations into the seed sector rather than "protecting" the informal seed supply system.

While the private sector supports minimal government intervention in their business, they also lobby hard to receive the necessary government protection to maximise and protect their profits: protection of their intellectual property rights over a variety or gene (PVP or patents) and, now with the Seed Bill, protection of their market to trade in seeds on their own terms.

Bill into an Act

India is seen as one the biggest markets in the world and as a result there is huge pressure on the government to adopt the Seed Bill and turn it into an Act. The Seed Bill is just one of the legislative changes in India to open up its markets and harmonise its laws with rich countries. These include amendments to the country's patent law and the model Agricultural Produce Marketing law. With the ongoing Parliament Session having concluded, the passage of the Bill has now been postponed to the next session (in July 2005). Meanwhile, the report of the Parliamentary Committee reviewing the Bill is awaited. Whenever the Bill is re-tabled, its rejection is unlikely without many voices of protest – the question is whether enough noise can be made about the Seed Bill, and whether these protests will go unheard.

11

India's Plant Variety Protection and Farmers' Rights Act

The Indian Parliament has finally passed the Plant Variety Protection and Farmers' Rights Bill. India has now, for the very first time, put in place a law to grant Plant Breeders' Rights on new varieties of seeds. The law also grants Farmers' Rights. These have been included in the legislation as a result of the determined and sustained campaign by NGOs, spearheaded by the Gene Campaign.

Gene Campaign's position right from the start was that if the status quo had to be changed and India had to grant Plant Breeders' Rights, our legislation would have to grant a strong Farmers' Rights at the same time. We maintained that 'plant back rights', i.e. the right to save seed from the harvest to sow the next crop, were no rights, only exemptions. Breeders under UPOV granted such exemptions, referred to as Farmers' Privilege. We insisted that Indian law had to grant rights, not provide exemptions, to its farmers.

Our key demand was for the farmer to retain the right to sell seed to other farmers, even if the variety was protected by a Breeders' Right. This right to sell seed is crucial to maintaining the livelihood basis of the farming community and the nation's self-reliance in agriculture. The clause on the right to sell seed was the major bone of contention to the very end of the legislative process. The pivotal importance of the farmer having the right to sell seed has to be seen in the context of seed production in India, where the farming community is the largest seed producer, providing about 87 percent of the country's annual requirement. Denying the farmer the right to sell seed would displace the farming community as the country's major seed provider. Their only replacement would be the 'life science' corporations since budget cuts have seriously weakened the capacity and output of the other major player, the public research institution. Any development that would give multinational corporations a significant share in seed production in India was unacceptable to civil society groups.

Farmers' Rights

In section 39 (iv) of the chapter on Farmers' Rights, the right to sell seed - even protected seed - has finally been provided

> The farmer shall be deemed to be entitled to save, use, sow, resow, exchange, share or sell his farm produce including seed of a variety protected under this Act in the same manner as he was entitled before the coming into force of this Act.

However, the farmer is not entitled to sell 'branded seed of a variety protected under this Act' (editor's italics).

Other Kinds of Farmers' Rights

The Act acknowledges the role of rural communities as contributors of landraces and farmer varieties in the breeding of new plant varieties. Breeders wanting to use farmers' varieties for creating Essentially Derived Varieties (EDVs) can not do so without the express permission of the farmers. Anyone can register a community's claim and have it duly recorded at a notified center. If the claim is found to be genuine, a share of profits made from the new variety has to go into a National Gene Fund.

Exemption from fees: Further protecting farmers from the new set of provisions being put in place, the new Act stipulates that farmers wishing to examine documents and papers or receive copies of rules and decisions made by the various authorities will be exempt from paying any fees.

Disclosure: Explicit and detailed disclosure in the passport data about the parentage of the new variety is required. If concealment is detected in the passport data, the Breeders certificate stands to be cancelled.

No terminator technology: Breeders must to submit an affidavit that their variety does not contain a Gene Use Restricting Technology (GURT) or terminator technology.

Protection against innocent infringement: Rightly assuming that farmers may unknowingly infringe Breeders' Rights since they will not be used to the new situation, the law provides for protection from prosecution for innocent infringement.

Good Clauses that Could Do Better

Benefit-sharing: The provision for payment for use of farmer varieties is welcome but modalities of implementing benefit-sharing must be made simpler and less bureaucratic. The revenues earned should only be available for use by farming communities, in the way that they decide.

Protection against bad seed: The clause protecting the farmer from spurious seed leaves too much to the discretion of the Authority. There should be specific guidelines, such as that compensation should amount to at least twice the projected harvest value of the crop. In addition, a jail term should be provided for repeated offence.

Rights of Breeders and Researchers

Breeders' Rights are fully protected by the legislation. On registration, the breeder has complete rights of commercialisation for the registered variety. These include the right to produce, sell, market, distribute, import or export the registered variety.

Penalties for infringing Breeders' Rights: Violation of a Breeders' Right can apply to the variety itself, as well as to its packaging. Penalties can range from Rs. 50,000 to ten lakh as well as a jail term ranging from three months to two years, depending on the severity of the damage caused. For repeated offence, fines can go upto Rs. 20 lakh and the jail term to three years.

The new law has provisions for Researchers' Rights which allow scientists and breeders free access to registered varieties for research. The registered variety can also be used for the purpose of creating new varieties. This flexibility is curtailed only when the registered variety needs to be used repeatedly as a parental line for commercial production of another variety.

Protection of Public Interest

The legislation includes public interest clauses, like exclusion of certain varieties from protection and the grant of compulsory licensing. To safeguard public interest, certain varieties may not be registered if it is felt that prevention of commercial exploitation of such variety is necessary to 'protect order or public morality or human, animal and plant life and health or to avoid serious prejudice to the environment'.

Compulsory licenses: The grant of a compulsory license is provided for if it is shown that the reasonable requirements of the public for seeds have not been satisfied or that the seed of the variety is not available to the public at a reasonable price. The breeder may file an opposition but should the charge be valid, the breeder can be ordered to grant a compulsory license under certain conditions, including the payment of a reasonable license fee. However, no compulsory license will be awarded if the Breeder can demonstrate reasonable grounds for his inability to produce the seed.

After Plant Variety Legislation, What Next?

Now that we have enacted a Plant Variety Protection and Farmers' Rights law, the next step will be to decide through which international platform India will interact with other nations. At present the only international platform is the UPOV, a Western platform regulating Plant Breeders' Rights for the industrial nations, and controlled by the life science corporations.

India Should Not Join UPOV

Gene Campaign opposes India's joining UPOV because UPOV does not address our needs and because its working is totally alien to the conditions of agriculture prevailing in the countries of the South. We believe that developing countries must create their own platform, which will grant Farmers' Rights distinct from Breeders' Rights, and be geared to work towards food and nutritional security in our countries. There is no concept of Farmers' Rights in the UPOV system, rights are granted only to the breeder, which in today's context means the seed companies. UPOV laws are formulated by industrial, not agricultural economies. In these countries the farming community is by and large rich and constitutes from two to five percent of the population. These countries do not have the large numbers of small and marginal farmers that we do.

CoFaB, a Developing Country Alternative to UPOV

Gene Campaign, along with Centre for Environment and Agriculture Development, has drafted an alternative treaty to UPOV to provide a forum for developing countries to implement their Farmers' and Breeders' Rights. This treaty is called the Convention of Farmers and Breeders, CoFaB for short. CoFaB reflects developing country strengths and vulnerabilities and seeks to secure their interests in agricultural policy-making.

The UNDP Human Development Report 1999 commended CoFaB as a 'strong and coordinated international proposal which offers developing countries an alternative to following European legislation by focusing legislation on need to protect farmers' rights to save and reuse seed and to fulfil the food and nutritional security goals of their people. Gene Campaign's purpose in drafting an alternative to UPOV was to provide the basis for a discussion on what kind of non-UPOV platform developing countries should have. Once consensus emerges after comprehensive analysis and critique among developing countries, it will not take long to come up with a minimum operational framework with which to start.

Environment-Related Trade Implications

Although WTO membership will provide opportunities to increase exports and many sectors are likely to benefit from it, these same sectors will face challenges from increasingly stringent environmental standards and various voluntary measures. Textiles, toys, leather, other light industry products and many agricultural goods are most likely to encounter environmental measures from western countries where consumers are more environmentally conscious.

Meanwhile, if imports of forest and food products grow, the chance to bring in alien invasive species will also increase. In order to protect human, plant and animal health and the environment, China needs to strengthen its sanitary and phytosanitary regulatory regime.

A high degree of policy preparedness will be necessary to enhance policy and administrative capacity to address the issues above.

First, it is imperative for China to adjust its environmental policy to address the consequences brought about by structural changes due to WTO membership. As changes in the economy will largely define the environmental agenda, more thorough assessments of the environmental consequences of WTO accession should be undertaken to ensure that the necessary policies are in place to address environmental challenges of trade liberalisation and to promote sustainable trade. Policy guidance is needed to seize the opportunity that China's WTO accession provides to address environmental problems through restructuring. WTO membership may also bring excellent opportunities for China to gradually upgrade its environmental management systems and standards.

Second, China needs to make efforts to comply with its WTO obligations. WTO rules will limit the options available to public authorities to respond to changes in environmental threats since any measures that are adopted must be both non-discriminatory and comply with the transparency provisions in various WTO

Agreements. To increase predictability and transparency, China must codify existing practices into written laws and regulations.

Third, China must integrate environmental concerns into relevant trade policies to address challenges both at home and abroad. Close cooperation will be necessary among departments responsible for trade, environment and technical standards, and others. "Green" measures in foreign countries should be studied to help enterprises meet the green challenge in international markets.

Fourth, there is a need to support Chinese officials in acquiring in-depth understanding of WTO rules related to trade and the environment and the policy issues involved. This will help them participate in future WTO negotiations, assist in the adoption of domestic rules consistent with WTO rules addressing trade and environmental issues, as well as resolve disputes within China's jurisdiction, at the bilateral level and under WTO auspices.

Finally, China's accession will bring changes in the "balance of power" between developed and developing countries in the WTO. As a participant in WTO decision-making and negotiations, China needs to develop a forward-looking and positive position in order to play an active role in promoting both trade liberalisation and sustainable development.

12

The Seeds Bill, 2004

A bill to provide for regulating the quality of seeds for sale, import and export and to facilitate production and supply of seeds of quality and for matters connected therewith or incidental thereto.

BE it enacted by Parliament in the Fifty-Fifth Year of the Republic of India as follows:-

Preliminary

Short title, extent, application and commencement.

1. (1) This Act may be called the Seeds Act, 2004.

   (2) It extends to the whole of India .

   (3) Save as otherwise provided in this Act, it shall apply to-

      (a) every dealer; and

      (b) every producer of seed except when the seed is produced by him for his own use and not for sale.

   (4) It shall come into force on such date as the Central Government may, by notification, appoint.

Definitions

2. In this Act, unless the context otherwise requires,

(1) "agriculture" includes horticulture, forestry and cultivation of plantation, medicinal and aromatic plants;

(2) "Central Seed Testing Laboratory" means the Central Seed Testing Laboratory established or declared as such under sub-section (1) of section 32;

(3) "Certification Agency" means an agency established under section 26 or accredited under section 27 or recognised under section 30;

(4) "Chairperson" means the Chairperson of the Committee;

(5) "Committee" means the Central Seed Committee constituted under sub-section (1) of section 3;

(6) "container" means a box, bottle, casket, tin, barrel, case, receptacle, sack, bag, wrapper or other thing in which any article or thing is placed or packed;

(7) "dealer" means a person who carries on the business of buying and selling, exporting, or importing seed, and includes an agent of a dealer;

(8) "export" means taking out of India by land, sea or air;

(9) "farmer" means any person who cultivates crops either by cultivating the land himself or through any other person but does not include any individual, company, trader or dealer who engages in the procurement and sale of seeds on a commercial basis;

(10) "horticulture nursery" means any place where horticulture plants are, in the regular course of

business, produced or propagated and sold for transplantation;

(11) "import" means bringing into India by land, sea or air;

(12) "kind" means one or more related species or sub-species of crop plants each individually or collectively known by one common name such as cabbage, maize, paddy and wheat;

(13) "member" means a member of the Committee;

(14) "misbranded" - A seed shall be deemed to be misbranded if-

(i) it is a substitute for, or resembles in a manner likely to deceive, another variety of seed under the name of which it is sold, and is not plainly and conspicuously labelled so as to indicate its true nature;

(ii) it is falsely stated to be the product of any place or country;

(iii) it is sold by a name which belongs to another kind or variety of seed;

(iv) false claims are made for it upon the label or otherwise;

(v) when sold in a package which has been sealed or prepared by, or at the instance, of the dealer and which bears his name and address, the contents of each package are not conspicuously and correctly stated on the outside thereof within the limits of variability prescribed under this Act;

(vi) the package containing it, or the label on the package bears any statement, design or device regarding the quality or the kind or variety of seed contained therein, which is false or misleading in any material particular or if the package is otherwise deceptive with respect to its contents;

(vii) it is not registered in the manner required by or under this Act;

(viii) its label contains any reference to registration other than the registration number;

(ix) its label does not contain a warning or caution which may be necessary, and sufficient, if complied with, to protect human, animal and plant life and health or to avoid serious prejudice to the environment;

(x) the package containing it or the label on the package bears the name of a fictitious individual or company as the dealer of the kind or variety; or

(xi) it is not labelled in accordance with the requirements of this Act or the rules made thereunder;

(15) "notification" means a notification published in the Official Gazette;

(16) "prescribed" means prescribed by rules made under this Act;

(17) "producer" means a person, group of persons, firm or organisation who grows or organises the production of seeds;

(18) "registered kind or variety", in relation to any seed, means any kind, or variety thereof, registered under section 13;

(19) "Registration Sub-Committee" means the Registration Sub-Committee constituted under sub-section (1) of section 7;]

(20) "regulation" means a regulation made by the Committee under this Act;

(21) "seed" means any type of living embryo or propagule capable of regeneration and giving rise to a plant of agriculture which is true to such type;

(22) "Seed Analyst" means a Seed Analyst appointed under section 33;

(23) "Seed Inspector" means a Seed Inspector appointed under section 34;

(24) "seed processing" means the process by which seeds and planting materials are dried, threshed, shelled, ginned or delinted (in cotton), cleaned, graded or treated;

(25) "spurious seed" means any seed which is not genuine or true to type;

(26) "State Government" ,in relation to a Union territory, means the administrator thereof;

(27) "State Seed Testing Laboratory", in relation to any State, means the State Seed Laboratory established or declared as such under sub-section (2) of section 32 for that State;

(28) "transgenic variety" means seed or planting material synthesised or developed by modifying or altering the genetic composition by means of genetic engineering;

(29) "variety" means a plant grouping except micro-organism within a single botanical taxon of the lowest known rank, which can be

(i) defined by the expression of the characteristics resulting from a given genotype of that plant grouping;

(ii) distinguished from any other plant grouping by expression of at least one of the said characteristics; and

(iii) considered as a unit with regard to its suitability for being propagated, which remains unchanged after such propagation,and includes propagating material of such variety, extant variety, transgenic variety, farmers' variety and essentially derived variety.Footnote: "essentially derived variety", in respect of a variety (the initial variety) shall be said to be essentially derived from such initial variety when it-

(a) is predominantly derived from such initial variety, or from a variety that itself is predominantly derived from such initial variety, while retaining the expression of the essential characteristics that result from the genotype or combination of genotypes of such initial variety;

(b) is clearly distinguishable from such initial variety; and

(c) conforms (except for the differences which result from the act of derivation) to such initial variety in the expression of the essential characteristics that result from the genotype or combination of genotypes of such initial variety;

Extant variety - "extant variety" means a variety available in India which is-

(a) notified under section 5 of the Seeds Act, 1966; or

(b) farmers' variety as defined in PVP Act; or

(c) a variety about which there is common knowledge; or

(d) any other variety which is in public domain.

The Central Seed Committee, Registration and Other Sub-Committees

Constitution of Central Seed Committee

3. (1) The Central Government shall, by notification, constitute, for the purpose of this Act, a Committee to be called the Central Seed Committee.

Composition of the Committee

4.(1) The Committee shall consist of a Chairperson, members, ex-officio and other members, to be nominated by the Central Government.

(2) The Secretary to the Government of India in the Department of Agriculture and Co-operation, Ministry of Agriculture, shall be Chairperson, ex officio.

(3) The Committee shall consist of the following members, ex officio namely:-

(i) the Agriculture Commissioner, Department of Agriculture and Co-operation, Government of India ;

(ii) the Deputy Director General (Crop Sciences), Indian Council of Agricultural Research;

(iii) the Deputy Director General (Horticulture), Indian Council of Agricultural Research;

(iv) the Joint Secretary in charge of seeds in the Department of Agriculture and Co-operation, Government of India

(v) the Horticulture Commissioner, Department of Agriculture and Co-operation, Government of India;

(vi) a representative of the Department of Bio-technology, Government of India, not below the rank of Joint Secretary to the Government of India;

(vii) a representative of the Ministry of Environment and Forests, Government of India, not below the rank of Joint Secretary to the Government of India.

(4) The Committee shall consist of the following other members to be nominated by the Central Government, namely:-

(i) the Secretary (Agriculture) from five States, one each from three out of the five geographical zones of the country as mentioned in the Schedule on rotation basis;

(ii) Director, State Seed Certification Agency from one State which is not represented under clause (i);

(iii) Managing Director, State Seeds Corporation, from one State which is not represented under clause (i) or clause (ii);

(iv) two representatives of farmers;

(v) two representatives of seed industry;

(vi) two specialists or experts in the field of seed development.

(5) The Committee may associate with it, in such manner, on such terms and for such purposes as it may deem fit, any person whose assistance or

advice it may desire in complying with any of the provisions of this Act, and a person so associated shall have the right to take part in the discussion of the Committee relevant to the purposes for which he has been associated, but shall not have the right to vote and shall be entitled to receive such allowances or fees as may be fixed by the Central Government.

(6) A Member nominated under sub-section (5) shall, unless his seat becomes vacant earlier by resignation, death or otherwise, be entitled to hold office for two years from the date of his nomination but shall be eligible for re-nomination provided that the said member shall hold office only for so long as he holds the appointment by virtue of which his nomination was made.

(7) Save as otherwise provided, the terms and conditions of service of the members shall be such as may be prescribed.

(8) A member other than an ex officio member may resign his office by giving notice in writing to the Central Government and on such resignation being accepted, he shall be deemed to have vacated his office.

(9) A person shall be disqualified for being nominated or appointed as a member if he-

(i) has been convicted and sentenced to imprisonment for an offence which, in the opinion of the Central Government, involves moral turpitude; or

(ii) is an undischarged insolvent; or

(iii) is of unsound mind and stands so declared by a competent court.

(10) No act or proceeding of the Committee shall become invalid merely by reason of -

(i) any vacancy therein, or any defect in the constitution thereof; or

(ii) any defect in the appointment of a person acting as the Chairperson or a member of the Committee; or

(iii) any irregularity in the procedure of the Committee not affecting the merits of the case.

(11) The Central Government may, at any time, remove from office any member other than member, ex-officio after giving him a reasonable opportunity of showing cause against the proposed removal.

Powers and functions of the Committee

5. The Committee shall be responsible for and shall have all the powers for the effective implementation of this Act and shall advise the Central Government and the State Governments on matters relating to-

(a) seed programming and planning;

(b) seed development and production;

(c) export and import of seeds;

(d) standards for registration, certification and seed testing;

(e) seed registration and its enforcement;

(f) such other matters as may be specified by the Central Government.

Powers of Committee to specify minimum limits of germination, purity, seed health, etc.

6. The Committee may, by notification, specify-

(a) the minimum limits of germination, genetic and physical purity, and seed health, with respect to any seed of any kind of variety;

(b) the mark or label to indicate that such seed conforms to the minimum limits of germination, genetic and physical purity, and seed health specified under clause (a), and other particulars, such as expected performance of the seed in accordance with the information provided by the producer under section 14 which such mark or label may contain.

Registration and other Sub-Committees of the Committee and their functions

7.(1) The Committee shall constitute a Sub-Committee to be called the Registration Sub-Committee consisting of a Chairman and such number of other members, to assist him in the discharge of the functions of the Committee, as may be prescribed.

(2) It shall be the duty of the Registration Sub-Committee-

(a) to register seeds of varieties after scrutinising their claims as made in the application in such manner as may be prescribed;

(b) to perform such other functions as are assigned to it by the Committee.

(3) The Committee may appoint as many other Sub-Committees including a Sub-Committee on Seed Certification as it deems fit consisting wholly of the members of the Committee or wholly of other persons or partly of members of the Committee and partly of other persons as it thinks fit to exercise such powers and perform such duties as may be delegated to them.

Procedure of the Committee and its Sub-Committees

8. The Committee may, subject to the previous approval of the Central Government, make regulations for the purpose of regulating its own procedure and the procedure of any Sub-Committee thereof.

Secretary and other officers of the Committee

9. The Central Government shall -

(a) appoint a person to be the Secretary of the Committee; and

(b) provide the Committee with such technical and other officers and employees as may be necessary for the efficient performance of the functions of the Committee under this Act.

Meetings of the Committee

10.(1) The Committee shall meet as and when necessary at such time and place and shall observe such procedure in regard to transaction of business at its meetings (including the quorum at meetings) as may be provided by regulations.

(2) The Chairperson or, in his absence, the Agricultural Commissioner or, in the absence of both the Chairperson and the Agriculture Commissioner, any member chosen by the members present from amongst themselves, shall preside at a meeting of the Committee.

(3) All questions at a meeting of the Committee shall be decided by a majority of votes of the members present and voting and in the case of an equality of votes, the Chairperson or, in his absence, the Agriculture Commissioner or, in the absence of

both the Chairperson and the Agriculture Commissioner the person presiding shall have and exercise a second or casting vote

State Seed Committee

11. Every State Government shall establish a State Seed Committee to -

(a) advise the Committee on registration of regional or local seeds of any kind or variety;

(b) advise the State Government on registration of seed producing units, seed processing units, seed dealers and horticulture nurseries;

(c) maintain, in each district, a list of seed dealers, seed producers, seed processing units and horticulture nurseries;

(d) seek information from persons engaged in the production, supply, distribution, trade or commerce in seeds of any kind or variety regarding stocks, prices, sales and other information in the manner as may be prescribed;

(e) advise the State Government and the Committee on all matters arising out of the administration and implementation of this Act; and

(f) carry out other functions assigned to, by, or under this Act.

Registration of Kinds and Varieties of Seeds, Etc.

Maintenance of National Register of seeds of kinds and varieties

12.(1) For the purposes of this Act, a register of all kinds and varieties of seed to be called the National Register of Seeds shall be kept by the Registration Sub-Committee wherein all specifications, as may be prescribed, shall be maintained.

(2) Subject to the directions of the Committee, the Register shall be kept under the control and management of the Registration Sub-Committee.

(3) The Registration Sub-Committee shall, within such intervals and in such manner as it thinks appropriate, publish the list of kinds and varieties of seed which have been registered during that interval.

Registration of seeds of any kind or variety

13.(1) No seed of any kind or variety shall, for the purpose of sowing or planting by any person, be sold unless such seed is registered under sub-section (2) by the Registration Sub-Committee in such manner as may be prescribed.

(2) Subject to the provisions of sections 14 and 15, the Registration Sub-Committee may register, or refuse any kind or variety of seed on the basis of information furnished by the producer on the results of multi-locational trials for such period as may be prescribed to establish the performance of that seed.

(3) The Registration Sub-Committee may grant provisional registration as prescribed to the varieties of seeds which are available in the market on the date of commencement of this Act.

(4) Registration made under this Act shall be valid for a period of fifteen years in the case of annual and biennial crops, and eighteen years for long duration perennials.

(5) At the expiry of the period granted under sub-section (4), the kind or variety of seed may be re-registered for a like period by the Registration Sub-Committee on the basis of information furnished by the producer on the results of such trials as may be prescribed under sub-section (2) to re-establish performance of the kind or variety of seed.

(6) The Registration Sub-Committee shall have the power to issue such directions to protect the interests of a producer against any abusive act committed by any third party during the period between the date of filing of application for registration and the date of decision by the Committee on such application.

Procedure for registration

14.(1) Every application for registration under sub-section (1) section 13 shall be made in such form and contain such particulars and be accompanied by such fees as may be prescribed.

(2) On receipt of any such application for the registration of a kind or variety of seed, the Registration Sub-Committee may, after such enquiry as it deems fit and after satisfying itself that the kind or variety of seed to which the application relates conforms to the claims made by the importer or by the seller, as the case may be, as regards the efficacy of the kind or variety of seed and its safety to human beings and animals, register the kind or variety, as the case may, of the seed on such conditions as may be specified by it and allot a registration number thereto and issue a certificate of registration.

(3) The Registration Sub-Committee may, having regard to the efficacy of the seeds and its safety to human beings and animals, vary the conditions subject to which a certificate of registration has been granted and may, for that purpose, require the certificate holder by notice in writing to deliver the certificate to it within such time as may be specified in the notice.

Special provision for registration of transgenic varieties

15.(1) Notwithstanding anything contained in section 14, no seed of any transgenic variety shall be registered unless the applicant has obtained clearance in respect of the same as required by or under the provisions of the Environment (Protection) Act, 1986:

Provided that the Registration Sub-Committee may, subject to clearance under the said Act, grant provisional registration, for a period not exceeding two years on the basis of information furnished by the producer on the results of multi-locational trials in the prescribed manner.

(2) Save as otherwise provided in sub-section (1), the form and manner in which and procedure for registration of transgenic variety of seed and the fee payable thereto shall be the same as applicable in case of registration under section 14.

Cancellation of registration of seeds of kinds and varieties

16.(1) The Registration Sub-Committee may cancel any registration granted under section 13 or section 15 or any one or more of the following grounds, namely:-

(a) that the holder of the certificate has violated any of the terms and conditions of the registration; or

(b) that the registration has been obtained by misrepresentation or concealment of essential data; or

(c) that the variety is not performing in accordance with the information provided by the producer under sub-section

(3) of section 14 or has become obsolete or has outlived its utility; or(d) that prevention of commercial exploitation of such variety of seeds is necessary.

(i) in the public interest;

(ii) to protect public order or public morality; or

(iii) to protect human beings, animal and plant life and health to avoid serious prejudice to the environment.

(2) No order of cancellation of registration under this section shall be made unless the holder thereof or the affected person concerned has been given a reasonable opportunity of showing cause in respect of the grounds for such cancellation.

Notification of cancellation of registration of seeds of kinds and varieties

17. The Registration Sub-Committee shall notify the cancellation of registration of a seed of any kind or variety made under section 13 or any registration made under section 15 in the Official Gazette

Exclusion of certain kinds or varieties of seed from registration

18. Notwithstanding anything contained in this Act, no registration of any kind or variety of seed shall be

made under this Act, if prevention of commercial exploitation of such kind or variety is necessary to protect public order or public morality or human, animal or plant life and health, or to avoid serious prejudice to the environment.

(2) A kind or variety of seed containing any technology, which is harmful, or potentially harmful, shall not be registered.

Explanation.- For the purposes of this sub-section, the expression "technology" includes genetic use restriction technology and terminator technology.

Evaluation of performance

19. The Committee may, for conducting trials to assess performance, accredit centers of the Indian Council of Agricultural Research, State Agricultural Universities and such other organisations fulfilling the eligibility requirements as may be prescribed, to conduct trials to evaluate the performance of any kind or variety of seed.

Compensation to farmer

20. Where the seed of any registered kind or variety is sold to a farmer, the producer, distributor or vendor, as the case may be, shall disclose the expected performance of such kind or variety to the farmer under given conditions, and if, such registered seed fails to provide the expected performance under such given conditions, the farmer may claim compensation from the producer, distributor or vendor under the Consumer Protection Act, 1986.

Seed producers and seed processing units to be registered

21.(1) No producer shall grow or organise the production

of seed unless he is registered as such by the State Government under this Act.

(2) No person shall maintain a seed processing unit unless such unit is registered by the State Government under this Act.

(3) The State Government shall register a producer or seed processing unit if he or it meets the specifications prescribed by the Central Government in terms of infrastructure, equipment and qualified manpower.

(4) Every application for registration under sub-section (3) shall be made in such form and manner and shall be accompanied by such fee as may be prescribed.

(5) The State Government may, after making such enquiry and subject to such conditions as it thinks fit, grant a certificate for maintaining a seed producing or a seed processing unit in such form as may be prescribed.

(6) Every seed producing and processing units shall furnish periodic returns to the Seed Certification Agency in such form and at such time as may be prescribed on the quantity of seeds of different kinds or varieties processed by them.

(7) The State Government may, after giving the holder of certificate of registration under sub-section (1), or sub-section (2), as the case may be, suspend or cancel the registration if —

(a) such registration has been obtained by misrepresentation as to a material particular relating to the specification in terms of infrastructure, equipment or availability of qualified manpower; or

(b) any of the provisions of this Act or the rules made thereunder has been contravened.

Seed dealers to be registered

22.(1) Every person who desires to carry on the business of selling, keeping for sale, offering to sell, bartering, import or export or otherwise supply any seed by himself, or by any other person on his behalf shall obtain a registration certificate as a dealer in seeds from the State Government

(2) Every applicant for dealership under sub-section (1) shall be required to furnish information about seed stocks, sales and other related information as may be prescribed.

(3) Even application for registration under sub-section(1) shall be made in such form and manner and shall be accompanied by such fee as may be prescribed.

(4) The State Government may, after making such enquiry and subject to such conditions as it thinks fit, grant a certificate of registration as a dealer in seeds in such form as may be prescribed.

(5) Every dealer registered under this section shall furnish such information and returns regarding seed stocks, seed lots, expiry date of seed lots and other related information as may be prescribed to the State Government.

(6) The State Government may, after giving the dealer an opportunity of being heard, suspend or cancel a certificate granted under this Act if-

(a) such registration had been obtained by misrepresentation of any material fact;

(b) contravenes any of the provisions of this Act or the rules made thereunder.

Horticulture nursery to be registered

23.(1) No person shall conduct or carry on the business of horticulture nursery unless such nursery is registered with the State Government.

(2) Every application for registration under sub-section (1) shall be made in such form and contain such particulars and shall be accompanied by such fee as may be prescribed.

Duties of registration holders of horticulture nursery

24. Every person who is a holder of a registration of a horticulture nursery under section 23 shall-

(a) keep a complete record of the origin or source of every planting material and performance record of mother trees in the nursery;

(b) keep a layout plan showing the position of the root-stocks and scions used in raising the horticulture plants;

(c) keep a performance record of the mother trees in the nursery;

(d) keep the nursery plants as well as the parent trees used for the production or propagation of horticulture plants free from infectious or contagious insects, pests or diseases affecting plants.

(e) furnish such information to the State Government on the production, stocks, sales and prices of planting material in the nursery as may be prescribed.

Regulation of Sale of Seed and Seed Certification Agencies

Regulation of sale of seeds of registered kinds and varieties

25. No person shall himself, or by any other person on his behalf, carry on the business of selling, keeping for sale, offering to sell, bartering, import or export or otherwise supply any kind of seed of any registered kind or variety unless-

(a) such seed is identifiable as to its kind or variety;

(b) such seed conforms to the minimum limit of germination and genetic, physical purity, seed health specified under clause (a) of section 6;

(c) the container of such seed bears in the prescribed manner, the mark or label bearing the correct particulars thereof, specified under clause (b) of section 6;

(d) the container of such seed, in the case of transgenic varieties, bears a declaration to this effect as specified in sub-clause (2) of section 15;

(e) he complies with such other requirements as may be prescribed.

State Seed Certification Agency

26. The Committee may, in consultation with the State Government, by notification, establish a State Seed Certification Agency for the State to carry out the functions entrusted to the State Seed Certification Agency by or under this Act:

Accreditation of Seed Certification Agencies

27.(1) The Committee may in consultation with the State Government and the State Seed Committee, accredit-

(a) organisations to carry out certification, on the fulfillment of such criteria, as may be prescribed, or

(b) individuals or seed producing organisations to carry out self- certification, in such manner as may be prescribed.

(2) The accredited individuals and seed producing organisations shall be subject to such inspection and control of the Committee, the concerned State Government and State Seed Certification Agency, as may be prescribed.

(3) The accreditation may be withdrawn by the Committee, for reasons to be recorded in writing and after giving to the concerned organisation or individual, as the case may be, a reasonable opportunity of being heard.

Grant of certificate by the State Seed Certification Agency

28.(1) Any person selling, keeping for sale, offering to sell, bartering or otherwise supplying any seed of any registered kind or variety may, if he desires to have such seed certified by the State Seed Certification Agency, apply to that Agency for the grant of a certificate for the purpose.

(2) Every application under sub-section (1) shall be made in such form, shall contain such particulars and shall be accompanied by such fee as may be prescribed.

(3) On receipt of an application under sub-section (1), the State Seed Certification Agency may, after such enquiry as it thinks fit and after satisfying itself that the seed to which the application relates conforms to the prescribed standards, grant a certificate in

such form and on such conditions as may be prescribed:

Provided that such standards shall not be lower than the minimum limit of germination, genetic and physical purity specified for that seed under clause (a) of section 6.

Revocation of certificate

29. If the State Seed Certification Agency is satisfied, either on a reference made to it in this behalf or otherwise, that-

(a) the certificate granted by it under section 28 has been obtained by misrepresentation as to an essential fact; or

(b) the holder of the certificate has, without reasonable cause, failed to comply with the conditions subject to which the certificate has been granted or has contravened any of the provisions of this Act or the rules made thereunder,then, without prejudice to any other penalty to which the holder of the certificate may be liable under this Act, the State Seed Certification Agency may, after giving the holder of the certificate an opportunity of showing cause, revoke the certificate.

Recognition of seed certification agencies in foreign countries

30. The Central Government may, on the recommendation of the Committee and by notification, recognise any seed certification agency established in any foreign country, for the purposes of this Act.

Appeals

Appeals

31.(1) Any person aggrieved by a decision of the Registration Sub-Committee under section 14, section 16 or section 27 or of the State Seed Certification Agency under section 28 or section 29 may, within thirty days from the date on which the decision is communicated to him prefer an appeal to such authority (hereinafter referred to as the appellate authority) as the Central Government may think fit to constitute:

Provided that the appellate authority may entertain an appeal after the expiry of the said period of thirty days if it is satisfied that the appellant was prevented by sufficient cause from filing the appeal in time.

(2) An appellate authority shall consist of a single person or three persons as the Central Government may think fit, to be appointed by that Government.

(3) The form and manner in which an appeal may be preferred under sub-section (1), the fee payable for such appeal and the procedure to be followed by the appellate authority shall be such as may be prescribed.

(4) On receipt of an appeal preferred under sub-section (1), the appellate authority shall, after giving the appellant and the other party an opportunity of being heard, dispose of the appeal as expeditiously as possible.

Seed Analysis and Seed Testing

Central and State Seed Testing Laboratories

32.(1) The Central Government may, by notification,

establish a Central Seed Testing Laboratory or declare any seed-testing laboratory as the Central Seed Testing Laboratory to carry out the functions entrusted to the Central Seed Testing Laboratory by or under this Act in the prescribed manner

(2) The State Government may, in consultation with the Committee, and by notification, establish one or more State Seed Testing Laboratories or declare any seed testing laboratory in the Government or non-Government sector as a State Seed Testing Laboratory where analysis of seed of any kind or variety shall be carried out under this Act in the prescribed manner.

(3) Every Seed Testing Laboratory referred to in sub-section (1) shall have as many Seed Analysts as the Central Government may consider necessary.

(4) Every Seed Testing Laboratory referred to in sub-section (2) shall have as many Seed Analysts as the State Government may consider necessary.

Seed Analysts

33.(1) In case of the Central Seed Laboratory, the Central Government and in other cases the State Government may, by notification, appoint such persons as the Government thinks fit and having the prescribed qualifications to be Seed Analysts and define the local limits of their jurisdiction.

(2) Every Central Seed Testing Laboratory established or declared under sub-section (1) of section 32 and every State Seed Testing Laboratory established or declared under sub-section (2) of that section shall have as many Seed Analysts as the Central Government or the State Government, as the case may be, specify.

SeedInspectors

34.(1) The State Government may, by notification, appoint such persons as it thinks fit, having the prescribed qualifications, to be Seed Inspectors and define the areas within which they shall exercise jurisdiction.

(2) Every Seed Inspector shall be subordinate to such authority as the State Government may specify in this behalf.

Powers of Seed Inspectors

35.(1) The Seed Inspector may-

(a) take samples of any seed of any kind or variety from-

(i) any person selling such seed; or

(ii) any person who is in the course of conveying, delivering or preparing to deliver such seed to a purchaser or a consignee; or

(iii) a purchaser or a consignee after delivery of such seed to him;

(b) send such sample for analysis to the Seed Analyst of the area within which such sample has been taken;

(c) enter and search, at all reasonable times, with such assistance, if any, as he considers necessary, any place in which he has reason to believe that an offence under this Act has been or is being committed and order in writing the person in possession of any seed in respect of which the offence has been or is being committed, not to dispose of any stock of such seed for a specific period not exceeding thirty days or, unless the alleged offence is such that the defect may be removed by the possessor of the seed, seize the stock of such seed;

(d) examine any record, register, document or any other material object found in any place mentioned in clause (c) and seize the same if he has reason to believe that it may furnish evidence of the commission of an offence punishable under this Act; and

(e) exercise such other powers as may be necessary for carrying out the purposes of this Act or any rule or regulation made thereunder.

(2) The power conferred by this section includes the power to break-open any container in which any seed of any kind or variety may be contained or to break-open the door of any premises where any such seed may be kept for sale: Provided that the power to break-open the door shall be exercised only after the owner or any other person in occupation of the premises, if he is present therein, refuses to open the door on being called upon to do so.

(3) Where the Seed Inspector takes any action under clause (a) of sub-section (1), he shall, as far as possible, call not less than two persons to be present at the time when such action is taken and take their signatures on a memorandum to be prepared in such form and manner as may be prescribed.

(4) The provisions of the Code of Criminal Procedure, 1973, or in relation to the State of Jammu and Kashmir, the provisions of any corresponding law in force in that State, shall, so far as may be, apply to any search or seizure under this section as they apply to any search or seizure made under the

authority of a warrant issued under section 94 of the said Code, or, as the case may be, under the corresponding provisions of the said law.

EXport and Import of Seeds

Import of seeds

36.(1) All import of seeds -

(a) shall be subject to the provisions of the Plants, Fruits and Seeds (Regulation of Import into India) Order, 1989, or any corresponding order made under section 3 of the Destructive Insects and Pests Act, 1914;

(b) shall conform to minimum limits of germination, genetic and physical purity, and seed health as prescribed under section 6; and

(c) shall be subject to registration as may be granted on the basis of information furnished by the importer on the results of multi-locational trials for such period as may be prescribed to establish performance.

(2) The Central Government may, by notification, permit to import an unregistered variety in such quantity and subject to fulfilling such conditions as may be specified in that notification for research purposes.

Export of seeds

37. The Central Government may, on the advice of the Committee, restrict, by notification, the export of seeds of any kind or variety if it is deemed that such export may adversely affect the food security of the country, or if it is felt that the reasonable

requirements of the public will not be met, or on such other grounds as may be prescribed.

Offences and Punishment

Offences and punishment

38. If any person -

(a) contravenes any provision of this Act or any rule made thereunder; or

(b) imports, sells, stocks or exhibits for sale or barter; and or otherwise supplies any seed of any kind or variety deemed to be misbranded ; or

(c) imports, sells, stocks or exhibits for sale or barter, or otherwise supplies any seed of any kind or variety without a certificate of registration; or

(d) obstructs the Committee, Registration Sub-Committee or Seed Certification Agency or Seed Inspector or Seed Analyst or any other authority appointed or duly empowered under this Act in the exercise of its powers or discharge of their duties under this Act or the rules made thereunder,he shall, on conviction, be punishable - with fine which shall not be less than five thousand rupees but which may extend to twenty five thousand rupees.

(2) If any person sells any seed which does not conform to the standards of physical purity, germination or health or does not maintain any records required to be maintained under this Act or the rules made thereunder he shall, on conviction, be punishable with fine which shall not be less than

five thousand rupees but which may extend to twenty- five thousand rupees.

(3) If any person furnishes any false information relating to the standards of genetic purity, misbrands any seed or supplies any spurious seed or spurious transgenic variety, sells any non-registered seeds he shall, on conviction be punishable with imprisonment for a term which may extend to six months or with fine which may extend to fifty thousand rupees or with both.

Forfeiture of property

39. When any person has been convicted under this Act for the contravention of any of the provisions of this Act or the rules made thereunder, the seed in respect of which the contravention has been committed shall be forfeited to the Central Government.

Offences by companies

40.(1) Where an offence under this Act has been committed by a company, every person who at the time the offence was committed was in charge of, and was responsible to the company for the conduct of the business of the company, as well as the company, shall be deemed to be guilty of the offence and shall be liable to be proceeded against and punished accordingly:

Provided that nothing contained in this sub-section shall render any such person liable to any punishment under this Act if he proves that the offence was committed without his knowledge and that he exercised all due diligence to prevent the commission of such offence.

(2) Notwithstanding anything contained in sub-section (1), where an offence under this Act has been committed by a company and it is proved that the offence has been committed with the consent or connivance of, or is attributable to any neglect on the part of, any director, manager, secretary or other officer of the company, such director, manager, secretary or other officer shall also be deemed to be guilty of that offence and shall be liable to be proceeded against and punished accordingly.Explanation. - For the purpose of this section,-

(a) "company" means any body corporate and includes a firm or other association of individuals; and

(b) "director", in relation to a firm, means a partner in the firm.

Power of Central Government

Power of Central Government to give directions to the State Governments

41. The Central Government may give such directions to any State Governments as may appear to the Central Government to be necessary for carrying into execution in the State any of the provisions of this Act or of any rule made there under.

Power of Central Government to issue directions to the Committee

42.(1) Without prejudice to the foregoing provisions of this Act, the Committee shall, in the discharge of its functions and duties under this Act, be bound by such directions on questions of policy as the

Central Government may give in writing to it from time to time.

(2) The decision of the Central Government whether a question is one of policy or not shall be final.

Exemption from registration

43.(1) Nothing in this Act shall restrict the right of the farmer to save, use, exchange, share or sell his farm seeds and planting material, except that he shall not sell such seed or planting material under a brand name or which does not conform to the minimum limit of germination, physical purity, genetic purity prescribed under clause (a) or clause (b) of section 6.(2) The Central Government may, by notification, and subject to conditions, if any, as it may specify therein, exempt from all or any of the provisions of this Act or the rules made thereunder, any educational, scientific or research or extension organisation.

Miscellaneous

Protection of action taken in good faith

44. No suit, prosecution or other legal proceeding shall lie against the Government or any person for anything which is in good faith done or intended to be done under this Act.

Power to remove difficulties

45.(1) If any difficulty arises in giving effect to the provisions of this Act, the Central Government may, by order published in the Official Gazette, make such provisions not inconsistent with the provisions of this Act as may appear to be necessary for removing the difficulty:

Provided that no order shall be made under this section after the expiry of two years from the date of commencement of this Act.

(2) Every order made under sub-section (1) shall be laid before each House of Parliament.

Power of Central Government to make rules

46.(1) The Central Government may by notification, make rules to carry out the provisions of this Act.

(2) In particular and without prejudice to the generality of the foregoing power, such rules may provide for all or any of the following matters, namely:-

(a) the terms and conditions of service of members of the Committee under sub-section (7) of section 4;

(b) the matters to be specified under clause (f) of section 5;

(c) the functions of the registration sub-committee under sub-section (1) of section 7;

(d) the manner of scrutinising applications under clause (a) of sub-section (2) of section 7;

(e) the specifications which shall be maintained in the National Register of Seeds of kinds or varieties under sub-section (1) of section 12;

(f) the manner of registration of seed of any kind or variety under sub-section (1) and (3) of section 13;

(g) the period for which multi-locational trials shall be conducted under sub-section (2) of section 13;

(h) the form of application and the particulars which should be furnished in such application under sub-section (1) of section 14;

(i) the eligibility requirement which an organisation shall fulfil for accreditation under section 19;

(j) the specification required to be fulfilled for registration as a producer or seed producing unit under sub-section (3) of section 21;

(k) the form and manner in which an application for registration under sub-section (3) of section 21 shall be made and the fee with which such application shall be accompanied under sub-section (5) of said section 21;

(l) the form in which a certificate for maintaining a seed producing or seed processing unit may be granted under sub-section (5) of section 21;

(m) the form in which and time within which periodic returns shall be filled under sub-section (6) of section 21;

(n) the information which an application for dealership in seeds shall be furnished under sub-section (2) of section 22;

(o) the form and manner in which an application for registration as seed dealer under sub-section (1) of section 22 shall be made and the fee which shall accompany such application under sub-section (3) of that section;

(p) the form in which a certificate of registration as a dealer in seeds shall be granted under sub-section (4) of section 22;

(q) the information and return which a registered dealer shall furnish to the State Government under sub-section (5) of section 22;

(r) the form in which an application for registration of a horticulture nursery shall be made, the particulars which such application shall contain and fee which shall accompany such application under sub-section (2) of section 23;

(s) the information on production, stocks, sales and prices of planting material in a nursery shall be furnished to the State Government under section 24;

(t) the requirement which a person carrying on business of selling, etc. of any registered kind or variety of seeds shall comply with under clause (e) of section 25;

(u) the criteria to be fulfilled under clause (a) and the manner of carrying out self-certification under clause (b) of sub-section (1) of section 27;

(v) the inspection and control of the Committee, the concerned State Government and the State Seeds Certification Agency for accrediting individuals and seed producing organisations under sub-section (2) of section 27;

(w) the form of application and the particulars to be furnished in such application and the fee which shall accompany such application under sub-section (2) of section 28;

(x) the form in which and the conditions subject to which a certificate shall be granted under sub-section (3) of section 28;

(y) the form and manner in which an appeal shall be preferred and the fee which such appeal shall accompany under sub-section (3) of section 31;

(z) the manner in which a Central Seed Testing Laboratory established or declared under sub-section (1) of section 32 shall carry out its functions;

(za) the manner of carrying out analysis of seeds shall be made under sub-section (2) of section 32;

(zb) the qualifications which a person to be appointed as Seed Analysts shall possess under sub-section (1) of section 33;

(zc) the qualifications which a person to be appointed as Seed Inspector shall possess under sub-section (1) of section 34; (zc) the form and manner in which the memorandum shall be prepared under sub-section (3) of section 35;

(zd) the grounds on which the Central Government may restrict export of seeds under section 37; (ze) any other matter which is to be or may be prescribed.

Power of Committee to make regulations

47.(1) The Committee may, with the previous approval of the Central Government, by notification, make regulations not inconsistent with the provisions of this Act and the rules made thereunder, to provide for all matters for which provision is necessary or expedient for the purpose of giving effect to the provisions of this Act.

(2) In particular and without prejudice to the generality of the foregoing power, such regulations may provide for all or any of the following matters, namely:-

(a) the procedure for conduct of business to be transacted by the Committee or any Sub-Committee thereof under section 8;

(b) the procedure in regard to transaction of business at meetings of the Committee (including the quorum at meetings) under sub-section (1) of section 10.

Rules and regu-lations to be laid before Parliament

48. Every rule and every regulation made under this Act shall be laid as soon as may be after it is made, before each House of Parliament, while it is in session, for a total period of thirty days which may be comprised in one session or in two or more successive sessions, and if, before the expiry of the session immediately following the session or the successive sessions aforesaid, both Houses agree in making any modification in the rule or regulation or both Houses agree that the rule or regulation should not be made, the rule or regulation shall, thereafter, have effect only in such modified form or be of no effect, as the case may be; so, however, that any such modification or annulment shall be without prejudice to the validity of anything previously done under that rule or regulation.

Repeal and savings

49. On the commencement of this Act, the Seeds Act, 1966 shall stand repealed; Provided that such repeal shall not affect,-

(a) the previous operation of the law so repealed or anything duly done or suffered thereunder; or

(b) any right, privilege, obligation or liability acquired, accrued or incurred under the law so repealed; or

(c) any penalty, forfeiture or punishment incurred in respect of any offence committed against the Act so repealed; or

(d) any investigation, proceeding, legal proceeding or remedy in respect of any such right, privilege, obligation, liability, penalty, forfeiture or punishment as aforesaid; and any such investigation, proceedings, legal proceeding or remedy may be instituted, continued or enforced; any such penalty forfeiture or punishment may be imposed as if this Act had not been passed: Provided further that, subject to the first proviso and any saving provisions made elsewhere in this Act anything done, any action taken, any rule made, any notifications or orders issued under the provisions of the Act so repealed shall, in so far as they are not inconsistent with the provisions of this Act, be deemed to have been done, taken, made or issued under the corresponding provisions of this Act, and shall continue to be in force accordingly, unless and until expressly or implied repealed by any thing done, action taken, rules made or, notification or orders issued under this Act.(2)

Notwithstanding such repeals any kind or variety of seeds that has been notified under the law as so repealed shall be deemed to have been registered under this Act, and any seed certification agency established under section 18 of the Seeds Act, 1966 shall be deemed to have been established or recognised, as the case may be, under this Act.

The Schedule

[See section 4(4)(i),(ii) and (iii)]

Geographical Zones

Zone-I	Andhra Pradesh, Karnakata, Kerala, Lakshadweep, Pondicherry and Tamil Nadu.
Zone II	Andaman and Nicobar Islands, Bihar, Chhatisgarh, Jharkhand, Madhya Pradesh, Orissa and West Bengal.
Zone III	Arunachal Pradesh, Assam, Manipur, Meghalaya, Mizoram, Nagaland, Sikkim and Tripura
Zone IV	Dadra and Nagar Haveli, Daman and Diu, Goa, Gujarat, Rajasthan and Maharashtra.
Zone V	Chandigrah, Haryana, Himachal Pradesh, Jammu and Kashmir, National Capital Territory of DElhi, Punjab, Uttranchal and Uttar Pradesh

Bibliography

Butler, L.J. and Marion, B.W., *The Impacts of Patent Protection on the US Seed Industry and Public Plant Breeding*, N.C. Project 117, Monograph 16, Research Division, College of Agricultural and Life Sciences, University of Wisconsin-Madison, Madison, Wisconsin, 1985.

Clunies-Ross, T., "Creeping Enclosure: Seed Legislation, Plant Breeder's rights and Scottish Potatoes", *The Ecologist*, Vol. 26, No. 3 May/June, 1996.

Flynn S, Turner R.M, Dickie J.B, "Seed Information Database", October 2004.

Janis, Mark D., "Sustainable Agriculture, Patent Rights, and Plant Innovation", 9 *Ind. J. Global Legal Stud*, 91 2001.

Juma, C., *The Gene Hunters: Biotechnology and the Scramble for Seeds*, Princeton University Press: Princeton, 1989.

Kloppenberg, J., *Seeds and Sovereignty*, Duke University Press: London, 1988.

Kowalski, Stanley P. & R. David Kryder, "Golden Rice: A Case Study in Intellectual Property Management and International Capacity Building", *13 RISK* 47, 2002.

McEowen Roger A. & Neil E. Harl, "Key Supreme Court Ruling on Plant Patents", *13 Agric. L. Dig.* 9, 2002.

McGarity, Thomas O., "Seeds of Distrust: Federal Regulation of Genetically Modified Foods", 35 U. Mich. J.L. Reform 403, 2002.

Mooney, P.R., "The law of the seed: another development and plant genetic resources", *Development Dialogue*, 1983.

Mooney, Pat, "The Law of the Seed", *Development Dialogue*, Zed Books, Ltd.: London, 1983.

Ohlgart, Samantha M., Note, "The Terminator Gene: Intellectual Property Rights vs. the Farmers' Common Law Right to Save Seed", 7 Drake J. Agric. L. 473, 2002.

Wilkes, H.G., "Plant genetic resources over ten thousand years: from a handful of seed to the crop-specific mega-genebanks", *In Seeds and sovereignty: the use and control of plant genetic resources* (J.R. Kloppenburg, ed.), Duke University Press, London, 1988.

Index